Advance

PARENTING ON A PRAYER is a gift and a blessing. It is a gift to anyone who wants to be a better parent, more attentive, more supple, and able to be truly present for their children or grandchildren. And it is a blessing because it invites a kind of mindfulness and generosity of spirit that can blossom into love. This precious book embraces us and our children in wisdom, compassion, and joy.

—**Rabbi Bradley Artson,** Dean of the Ziegler School of Rabbinic Studies, author, *God of Becoming and Relationship: The Dynamic Nature of Process Theology*

PARENTING ON A PRAYER is a gift for every parent to have and to share. Rabbi Amy Grossblatt Pessah is a master teacher who brings Jewish prayers to life and reveals the inner wisdom of our tradition. Every page of this inspiring work is filled with lessons to live by. Parenting is the greatest gift of life, but also the most challenging and humbling. This remarkable book offers us encouragement through difficult times and perspective when life spins out of control. Most of all, it reminds us that something as simple as a prayer can transform the way we raise our children in blessings and in love.

—**Rabbi Naomi Levy,** spiritual leader of Nashuva and the author of *Einstein and the Rabbi*

In PARENTING ON A PRAYER, Rabbi Amy Grossblatt Pessah displays great depths of understanding and wisdom. She draws meaningfully on the Jewish prayer book as well as her own life as a mother to offer a realistic, comforting, and inspiring portrait of what it means to be a parent as one's children evolve and grow. Rabbi Grossblatt Pessah has provided a compassionate work of spiritual insight that will touch and direct the souls of all who read her. This is an important book for all who struggle and rejoice in the challenges of parenthood!

— **Rabbi David Ellenson**, Chancellor Emeritus of Hebrew Union College-Jewish Institute of Religion

PARENTING ON A PRAYER describes Rabbi Amy Grossblatt Pessah's sensitive and carefully observed spiritual journey through mothering three children. Pessah offers prayers and sacred texts, as well as narrations of her own memories, to inform an ethically aware, compassionate, and gentle but firm parenting strategy. Her thesis is that parenting can be a spiritual practice in which we strive over and over to enact loving presence, patience, and wisdom. From tenderness to tension to tragedy, Pessah offers us a startlingly honest view of her own experiences and a lens through which to view daily family life. Parenting can often be lonely, and Pessah's journey and reflections will be a good companion for many who are struggling to parent children in a complex and changing world.

— **Rabbi Jill Hammer**, author, *The Jewish Book of Days*

A midrash tells us that, when the Israelites stood at Mt. Sinai hearing the voice of God, each person heard that voice in the way that s/he could best receive its message. The beautiful hymn, An'im Z'mirot, expresses the importance of receptivity with these words: "They saw You young, they saw You old, They saw You patient, they saw You bold."

Rabbi Grossblatt Pessah continues this tradition in this thoughtful, emotionally honest book. As a lifelong student and practitioner of Jewish prayer, I can attest to the validity and deeply personal way in which she brings a new level of meaning to the prayers Jews recite daily and weekly, a level which has always been there and which Rabbi Grossblatt Pessah uncovers. The application of sacred texts to the realities of daily parenting and, in so doing, making child-rearing a deeply spiritual practice, is in harmony with the significance Judaism gives to family.

I only wish this book had been available to me when I was actively parenting and recommend it to others wholeheartedly.

— **Rabbi Daniel Siegel,** Spiritual Director, ALEPH: Alliance for Jewish Renewal Canada, Editor, *Kol Koreh Siddur* and *Machzor*

This honest, loving, scholarly, and profound book is an ancient and modern guidebook to parenting and a reminder to parents everywhere of the tenderness and wisdom with which we are all held by the Divine. As a pediatrician I have read and reviewed many books on parenting. Among them PARENTING ON A PRAYER is completely unique. To read it is to be prepared to parent more wisely and recognize more fully that you yourself are a child of God.

— **Rachel Naomi Remen,** MD

Author, *Kitchen Table Wisdom* and *My Grandfather's Blessings*

Clinical Professor, Family and Community Medicine

University of California San Francisco (UCSF) School of Medicine

PARENTING
ON A
PRAYER

Ancient Jewish Secrets
for Raising Modern Children

Amy Grossblatt Pessah

Ben Yehuda Press
Teaneck, New Jersey

Published by Ben Yehuda Press
122 Ayers Court #1B
Teaneck, NJ 07666

http://www.BenYehudaPress.com

To subscribe to our monthly book club and support independent Jewish publishing, visit https://www.patreon.com/BenYehudaPress

ISBN13 978-1-934730-71-3

Library of Congress Cataloging-in-Publication Data

Names: Pessah, Amy Grossblatt, author.
Title: Parenting on a prayer: ancient Jewish secrets for raising modern children / Amy Grossblatt Pessah.
Description: Teaneck, New Jersey Ben Yehuda Press, [2020]. | Summary: "In Parenting on a Prayer, Rabbi Amy Grossblatt Pessah mines the Jewish prayer book for key values for thoughtful parenting, relating them to the lessons she learned as the mother of three children"-- Provided by publisher.
Identifiers: LCCN 2019057615 | ISBN 9781934730713 (paperback)
Subjects: LCSH: Parenting--Religious aspects--Judaism. | Child rearing--Religious aspects--Judaism. | Jewish religious education of children. | Pessah, Amy Grossblatt.
Classification: LCC BM725.4 .P47 2020 | DDC 296.7/4--dc23
LC record available at https://lccn.loc.gov/2019057615

20 21 22 / 10 9 8 7 6 5 4 3 2   20200411

Dedication

With each child the world begins anew.
—Midrash

To my three beautiful blessings who began the world anew:
Josef Lavi, z"l
Eitan Lavi
Bat-Ella Zahava

Contents

Invitation

I wish someone had taught me the prayer for parenting. What magic words did I need to utter in order to make everything unfold with ease? A few whispers muttered under my breath, or a loud shout at the top of my lungs to make my kids stop fighting would have been a godsend. Perhaps I just wasn't aware of a special incantation that would mend broken bones and heal broken hearts, for I would have prayed those words with desperation and deep intention if only they would have made my parenting journey easier.

But alas, we know there are no such words, wishes, or desires of the heart that can help us navigate parenting unscathed. Most of the time it feels like parenting doesn't have a prayer—literally and metaphorically! How many times did I ask myself, "Do I even stand a chance?"

And when my kids became teenagers, would I be fighting an uphill battle against peer pressure and social media? I felt truly doomed.

Not knowing where to turn when my first child arrived, I spoke with family and friends about their experiences and began frantically and furiously reading countless parenting books, hoping to find the "perfect parenting formula." The more I read, the more I realized that there wasn't just one perfect formula. Raising children is not like completing a math problem or a science experiment. With children there are way too many variables. Sometimes x + y = z and then sometimes "x" wakes up cranky and decides to become a "w" and the answer you get is certainly something other than "z"!

After many months of gleaning from the "experts," I decided that maybe I should try to trust myself. Maybe I actually knew more than I thought; maybe it was time to trust my own intuition instead of listening solely to others. That was an incredibly scary moment in my life, especially as a first-time parent. With great trepidation, I followed my instinct; to my surprise, the more I listened, the more confident I became in my parenting.

I came to understand the uniqueness of each of my children and the challenge of applying generic principles to them. And yet, there was much wisdom to be gained from the experience, trials, and tribulations of others. How could I balance these two paths—an external collecting of information with my own internal intuitive knowing?

After two decades of searching, I have finally come to a place of integration; and now, I invite you to come along on my journey as I share how I found the answers to my question.

Introduction

"How could I balance these two paths—an external collecting of information with my own internal intuitive knowing?"

Having sought out numerous books on parenting, childrearing, and resiliency, imagine my surprise when my answer to this question came from what I consider to be an unlikely place—the Jewish prayer book. You might wonder, how could a book that most people don't understand or read actually provide wisdom and insights? How exactly can prayer be meaningful if we don't even know what we are saying? For most, the words of the prayer book are unfamiliar; for others, the prayers were simply memorized as children, in Hebrew, without a significant explanation provided. How precisely can we make sense of prayers written in an ancient cryptic language? And how, in God's name, can they actually shed light on parenting?

Jewish tradition teaches that when we are in the womb, a light burns above us, and we can see from one end of the world to the other. During that time, we are taught the entire Torah from beginning to end. But before we emerge, an angel comes and taps us on the top of our mouth and causes us to forget all that we learned. Hence, we are all born with that little indentation above our upper lips.* With that realization and recognition of all that we have forgotten, we begin to cry, and perhaps that is why babies emerge from the womb crying. It is a cry for the loss of all of our previous knowledge. We then spend the rest of our lives trying to rediscover all that we once knew.

So how do we begin to uncover what we once knew? I believe that by listening to our intuition or our "gut," we can come to uncover much of what we believed was hidden. In addition to following our instinct, there are other modalities, such as meditation and prayer that can help us listen more deeply to our inner selves. These tools can lead us on our journey of remembering and collecting what we once knew. Uncovering information for ourselves is valuable and intriguing; but when we become parents, the importance of uncovering these layers becomes essential.

---

*Babylonian Talmud, Niddah 30b

One Saturday morning, I was at Shabbat services and actually had a few moments to pray, *sans* children. I was struck by how some of the words in the prayer book could be interpreted as great parenting advice. After my initial discovery, I began to look for new insights, week after week. By examining each prayer, and looking at God playing the role of parent, I was able to apply the words of these ancient prayers to my modern-day life.

This idea of seeing God as our parent originates from the very beginning of the Jewish people with the stories that we read in the Torah. One of the first and most striking stories for me is about the relationship between God and Adam and Eve. When Adam and Eve are in the Garden of Eden, they are told that they are allowed to eat from any tree, except from the Tree of Knowledge of Good and Evil. For those of you who have kids and for those of you who remember being a kid, you know exactly from which tree they decided to eat—of course, the one from which they were forbidden to eat! After eating from that tree, Adam and Eve hide in the garden. God then calls them to find out where they are, *Ayeka*—"Where are you?"* As if God really needed to ask!

Imagine hearing your child's hand in the cookie jar, the cookie jar from which you specifically told her not to eat. You call and say, "What are you doing?" The response, "Nothing." You look for your child and you can't seem to find her. "Where are you?" You yell in an attempt to locate her, but you know your own house intimately and, if you wanted to, you could waltz right over to where she was standing. So too, I believe, it is with God. As the ultimate parent, I believe that God knew what His children were doing, just like we know when our children are being sneaky. For me, this story is a great example of how the Divine can be seen as a parent looking after Her children.**

While using this model of God as Parent is helpful, it can also be limiting, as God is much more than just Parent. In the prayer book, God is referred to as Y-H-V-H, pronounced *Adonai*—Lord, *Melech*—ruler,

---

*Genesis 3: 1-9

**A note on gender. The Hebrew language does not have a gender neutral form; a word is either masculine or feminine. There are contemporary scholars and female rabbis who have rewritten many prayers to be more gender inclusive. In order not to limit God, I will be alternating between masculine and feminine God language.

Tzur—rock, Creator of the Universe, Healer, and Savior. These various names for God help us to understand another dimension, another aspect of God. Within these names, we find both imminent (close) and transcendent (far) monikers, each resonating differently. Every name is unique, and each name is True. In one of my favorite children's books, *In God's Name*, author Sandy Eisenberg Sasso weaves a marvelous tale about people who are trying to find the One, True name for God. She writes that the "artist who carved figures from the earth's hard stone called God, My Rock; the woman who cared for the sick called God, Healer; the young woman who nursed her newborn son called God, Mother and the young gentleman who held the hand of his baby daughter called God, Father."* Eisenberg Sasso concludes by letting us know that each name is True, and combined, all of our names for God make up the One, True name of God.

My personal favorite name for God, which appears in the book of Exodus, is "*Ehyeh Asher Ehyeh*, which can be translated as either "I am that I am" or "I will be that which I will be." God shares this name with Moses after Moses approaches the burning bush and God tells him to take the Israelite slaves out from Egypt. Moses questions God by asking, "Who am I that I should go to Pharaoh, and that I should take the children of Israel out of Egypt?" God tells Moses not to worry, that God will remain with him. Then Moses says to God, "Ok, so when I come to the children of Israel and tell them 'The God of your fathers has sent me to you' and they say to me, 'What is God's name?' What shall I tell them?" And then God utters those powerful, elusive words, tell them "*Ehyeh Asher Ehyeh*," that's what you can tell the children of Israel.** Somehow this doesn't quite seem like the answer for which Moses was looking.

And yet, I believe that the power and the genius of God revealing that name, *Ehyeh Asher Ehyeh*, lies in God's ability to be what each of us needs God to be at various times and moments in our lives. At the stage of life that I am in now, God for me is very much like a parent. When I study the words of the Torah, I am struck by the parallels between my relationship with my children and the relationship of God with the Children of Israel. One example that makes me smile is the case of *chukim*. In the Torah,

---

* *In God's Name*, by Sandy Eisenberg Sasso, Jewish Lights Publishing, 1994.
** Exodus 3:10-14

there are *mitzvot*, commandments, referred to as *chukim*, statutes, that don't seem very logical to us. Nonetheless, we are commanded to uphold them, and the reason is "because I [God] said so.'" How many times a day do I utter those words, "Because I said so, that's why."

While I have called out to God by many names, at this juncture in my life I am most drawn to this aspect of God as parent because it is where I am. When I read the words of the Torah and the words of the prayer book, I read it through my parenting lens. It is this particular point of view that prompted me to write this book—to share what I've learned and to ask you to go inside and listen to your own inner GPS—Great Parenting System.

The book is divided into eighteen chapters, each representing a different prayer in the prayer book and an associated value that I believe to be important in raising children. The number 18 was chosen purposefully to be representative of the Hebrew meaning behind the number 18. Each letter in Hebrew has a numerical value. The word *chai* has two letters: *chet* representing 8, and *yud* representing 10. Together, they make up the word *chai*, meaning life. Many of you may be familiar with the song from Fiddler on the Roof, *L'Chayim*, To Life. I believe that by working toward fulfilling each of these values, our children's lives and our families' lives will be enriched and filled with much life.

Each chapter has the same format. The prayer is written in both transliterated Hebrew and English, followed by personal stories and explanations of what I see as a major idea or theme hidden within the prayer."" Additionally, I use the words of the prayer book as a springboard for my own spiritual insights and commentaries on how we can use this idea to become better parents. I've added a sidebar filled with some activities that promote each value along with questions to consider.

And just as God asked Adam and Eve in the Garden of Eden, I ask you the same question: *"Ayeka*, where are you?"* Where are you in your parenting journey? How can you use these words to help uncover what

---

*One example of a חוק, chok (singular of חוקים) relates to the prohibition of wearing clothing that contains a mixture of linen and wool. Leviticus 19:19.

""In addition to my own translating, I consulted two prayer books: *Siddur Sim Shalom*, edited by Rabbi Jules Harlow and *Kol Koreh*, edited by Rabbi Daniel Siegel. Translations from *Siddur Sim Shalom* are in Calibri font, translations from Kol Koreh are in Gil Sans font.

you already know in the depths of your Being? As we all strive to raise respectful, caring, decent, thoughtful, sensitive, upright, honest children, my prayer for each of you is that you, too, will find meaning and guidance from the words of our ancient tradition. Once you have become familiar with the meaning behind each prayer, I encourage you to find your own interpretations. After many years of soaking in the words of the prayer book, I've come to believe that while parenting does not have *a* prayer, it does have *many* prayers, some of which are uttered using the words in the prayer book, and others that emerge from our hearts.

May the words of our lips and the meditations of our hearts be acceptable.

With blessings and gratitude to *Ehyeh Asher Ehyeh*,

Amy Grossblatt Pessah

September 2, 2019

Boca Raton, Florida

Blessings
(Mah Tovu)

א

Mah Tovu—
How good it is…

For a parent of three school-age children, life gets hectic; and at times, even frantic. Like most parents, I often feel like a broken record. I hear myself saying, "How many times do I have to tell you to pick up your laundry, hang up your towel, take out the recycling?" Being The Reminder is an exhausting job; on top of that, I have another job—The Referee. "I told you to stop hitting your brother!" "Stop teasing your sister!" There are times when I feel I am about to lose it and say something I will regret. I want to shout and curse. In the midst of my anger, I remind myself how lucky I am to have three healthy, beautiful, happy children. I look at them, in all of their "spiritedness," and think, "I should bless them, not curse them." In other words, I choose to focus on my blessings. This lesson comes directly from *"Mah Tovu,"* which teaches us to refocus on blessings. In the midst of our anger, how might we be able to find blessing?

The first sentence of this prayer comes from a verse in the book of Numbers.[*] *"Mah tovu ohalecha Ya'akov,"* "How goodly are your tents of Jacob, your dwelling places O Yisrael." When the King of Moab, Balak, wanted the Israelites cursed, he hired the prophet Bilaam to do his bidding. After many exciting twists in his journey, including an interaction with a talking donkey, Bilaam is so impressed with the Israelites' encampment that instead of cursing them, he blesses them. The Midrash[**] shares that the flaps on the Israelites' tents were opened in a way that provided respect and privacy for all the people. This is the backdrop of the *Mah Tovu*

---

[*] Numbers 24:5

[**] *Midrash* is a Hebrew term meaning explanation or interpretation. It can refer to a single explanation or it can refer to a body of literature that includes various books of *midrashim* (plural for *midrash*).

prayer: even in the midst of curse (or chaos), we can pause for a moment and try to focus on blessing.

The Hebrew root for blessing is ברך, *beit, resh, chaf,* which can be vocalized to read *"berech,"* knee. When we bless, we bow at the knees, in recognition that there is something greater than human beings. By prostrating ourselves, we submit that life is not just about our ego. We work to go inward, constricting ourselves and our egos, and accepting that there will be times in our lives that we will have to bend, be it to an authority figure, a situation, a boss, a parent, or even a child.

Often times, blessings emerge from the realization that we cannot always put ourselves first. Sometimes we need to put the needs of others first. As parents, when we discipline our children, we do so because we believe it to be in the best interest of our child. But is it? Maybe we are caught up in a power struggle and we don't want to concede. Maybe we don't want to look foolish reneging on our word. Do we know for sure what is in the best interest of our child or might we just assume that we know? Being "right" does not always make situations turn out "right"; however, being flexible may help us to see the blessing in the moment. By looking at situations from different perspectives, and listening deeply to one another, we may see something new or different that will open up the door, or the tent, to hidden blessings.

Ways to Refocus on Blessings

1) Make a silly face.
2) Count to 20 (10 is too short!).
3) Take a time-out.
4) Look in your child's eyes.
5) Think back to a great memory.
6) Take out old photo albums/pictures
and look at your child as a baby.
7) Come up with your own mantra that you
can recite during stressful times.

ב

Ohalecha Ya'akov mishk'notecha Yisrael.

Your tents O, **Jacob**, Your dwelling places, O, **Israel.**

When I was in college, I decided that I would not take my husband's
last name when I got married. I felt that my parents worked hard to raise
me, paid for college, and helped put me through graduate school. I wanted
to keep my family name as a way to show my gratitude to them. I wanted
them to get the credit for doing all the hard work (and now as a parent,
I realize how much more went into raising a child!). Well, as luck or fate
would have it, the person I fell in love with had a non-negotiable condi-
tion—whomever he married would have to take his name. Not agreeing
was a deal-breaker. In the end, love conquered, and I did agree to take
his name. I kept my maiden name as my middle name with no hyphen
and both my maiden name and my married name are on all of my legal
documents. After twenty-two years, I have come to see that my name has
evolved just as I have. I am no longer Amy Grossblatt. While I have all
of my memories of Amy Grossblatt, I am now Amy Grossblatt Pessah,
which comes with new experiences and new memories that we, together,
have created. Names and naming are important, hence my decision to
keep both of mine, but what I have really learned along the way is that
just as our names change and evolve, so do we as individuals.

When we read, "How lovely are your dwellings, people of *Jacob*, your
sanctuaries, descendants of *Israel*," we are connecting the idea of people
evolving through their names. Jacob was born with the name Jacob but
as he dreamed, traveled, matured, and wrestled with an angel, his name
was changed by God to the name Israel.* In this first line of *Mah Tovu*,
we read both of Jacob's names: Jacob and Israel. One represents his given
identity, the other represents his acquired or earned identity.

Each of us has chosen names for our children. Hopefully, they are
names that they are proud of and will grow into. They will go through

* Genesis 32:25-29

life and dream, travel, mature, and probably wrestle with some of their own "angels" and then, most likely, they will acquire or earn a new name. Their new name might come in the guise of an actual name change or a nickname or an addition of a name, but as parents we can remember that is the natural course of events. We can't hold onto our children forever. *Mah tovu* teaches us that people change, grow, and evolve over time but in the end, *mah tovu*, it is good.

ג

Va'ani berov chasdecha, avoh veitechah...
Adonai ahavti me'on beitecha.

In Your abundant loving-kindness, O God, let me
enter Your house...Adonai, I love Your house,
the place where Your glory dwells.

Each year on our anniversary, my husband and I have a tradition to re-watch our wedding video. The rabbi who married us speaks about the open walls of the chuppah, symbolizing how our home should be in the future. Thankfully, we both agreed that we wanted our home to be open to our family, friends, and community. We wanted the kind of home where *mi casa es su casa* (my house is your house)—if we're home, please stop by for a visit.

We also wanted to pass to our children the value of having an open home. We want them to feel comfortable bringing home friends, knowing that our home is always open and that it is filled with love and fun and, of course, yummy food. We read in *Mah Tovu*, "Your great love inspires me to enter Your house… God, I love your house, the palace of Your glory."

I want my children to know that their house is safe and fun and cool, another message that can be extracted from this prayer. As one of my girlfriends says, "I tell my kids that our home is one of the safest places in the world and that allows them to try new things, fail, start again, knowing it will all be OK." Having an open home allows kids to feel proud of themselves and their family. They can share their treasures and favorite games. Having an open home teaches our kids how to be good hosts and how to be welcoming. And of course, the secret that all parents know, having an open home provides us with more transparency, allowing us to see who our kids are hanging out with and what their interests are.

Ways to Open Up Your Home

1) Play games in your yard and invite the neighbors.
2) Try for playdates once a week.
3) Invite another family for Friday night dinner.
4) Hold a movie and popcorn night.
5) If possible, have at-home birthday parties.
6) Celebrate holidays and invite guests.
7) Find a family that is new to your
community and invite them over.

Blessing: Questions to Consider

1) What aspects of your life would you define as *tov*, good? Are there blessings you forget to notice? What aspects would you like to improve?
2) In what ways have you evolved over the years? Has your name changed, literally? Figuratively? How can you begin to prepare yourself for your child's name/identity change?
3) Are you comfortable with the level of openness in your home? If not, how can you make your house more open?

Choices

(Asher Yatzar)

א

Baruch atah Adonai, Eloheinu, Melech haOlam,
asher yatzar et ha'Adam b'chochmah.

Praised are you, Adonai our God, Ruler of the Universe,
who fashions the human body in wisdom.[*]

Having grown up in a typical house that trusted Western medicine, as
an adult I nevertheless began dabbling in Eastern medicine—homeopathy,
flower remedies, acupuncture, vitamins and herbs—and I became a be-
liever. When I married an ER doctor, our medical philosophies collided.
Many years ago I had a terrible case of vertigo, which lasted three months.
During that time, true to my nature, I was seeing both a traditionally
Western-trained ENT, as well as an acupuncturist. My ENT ordered a
special test where they blow hot air in your ears to simulate severe dizzi-
ness—don't ask! While preparing for the test, I started chatting with the
specialist, asking him how people get vertigo and if there are people who
are predisposed to vertigo. He shared that they don't know of any specific
predispositions, but there does seem to be a connection between kidney
problems and ear problems. He continued to explain that before the cells
differentiate to form our bodies as we know them, the future ear cells and
the future kidney cells emerge from the same stem cells.

"Wow!" I exclaimed.

Earlier in the week I had visited my acupuncturist, who shared that
in order to treat my vertigo, he was going to treat my kidneys. Hmmm,

---

[*] Rabbi Marcia Prager offers another powerful translation for the first six words of this
blessing: "A Fountain of Blessings are You, The Eternal-Breath-of-Life-Beyond-and-
Within, Divine Expansiveness Concentrated within our World, Channeling Creative
Power to Manifest as the Mystery of Consciousness becoming Time-Space." Prager,
Rabbi Marcia *The Path of Blessing*. Vermont: Jewish Lights Publishing, 1998.

OK, that's a bit weird, I thought. He continued to explain that in Chinese medicine, there is a very strong connection between the ears and the kidneys. How cool was that—another collision! A Western-trained specialist and an Eastern-trained doctor, each linking the ears to the kidneys. How our bodies are fashioned is truly amazing.

After my boyfriend (now husband) completed his course on histology, the study of cells, he remarked on how amazing it is that so many babies are born healthy. With the numerous steps and stages of cell divisions and permutations that must occur in order for a baby to be born with its body in working form, he was in awe of this incredibly complicated process.

From time to time, I still go back and look at the ultrasounds of my kids from when they were in utero and I never cease to be amazed. How a human being is formed is nothing short of a miracle.

Each time I read the *Asher Yatzar* prayer, I am struck with awe by how our bodies, in all of their intricacies, are fashioned. When I recite this prayer, *Asher Yatzar*, I am, each time anew, thanking God for the miracle of our bodies, "Praised are You, *Adonai* Our God, Ruler of the universe, fashioning the human body in wisdom."

ב

Asher Yatzar
—who fashions

The Hebrew word *yatzar* can be translated as "fashions." The Hebrew root of this word is יצר and it literally means *to create* or *to form*. On Yom Kippur there is a beautiful *piyyut*, poem, that pleads for God to show mercy upon us. In it, God is described as various artisans: a mason, an iron craftsman, a glassblower, a cloth draper, a metal smith, and a potter. We humans are compared to the various media used by these artisans. The prayer begs for God's mercy as we are compared to the stone, iron, glass, cloth, metal, and clay that rest in God's hands.

In this *piyyut*, the Hebrew word that is used to describe God as a potter is יוצר, which has the same root—*yod, tzadee, resh*—as the word in our prayer, *yatzar.* God literally forms us or fashions us, as a potter would work his clay.

> We are as clay in potter's hands
> He does contract She does expand
> So we are yours to shape at will
> We yield to you our passions still *

As someone who has taken pottery classes, I am particularly struck by this image. Working with clay is much more difficult than it seems. First, the potter has to make sure the consistency of the clay is correct and then wedge the clay to ensure removal of any air bubbles. Next, and perhaps most importantly, the clay must be centered on the wheel before working. Getting the clay centered on the wheel is no small feat. I always find that if I, myself, am not feeling centered, it is nearly impossible to center my clay. Inversely, the days on which I am most centered, I can work more easily. Then, the clay is worked with water and various other tools in order to shape and move it. For me, the clay does not always move as I expect it to. Once I start working, I am always amazed at how a form emerges, almost with a mind of its own. I may have wanted a vase but wound up with a small pitcher or I may have intended to throw a plate but wound up with a bowl. Nonetheless, I come to love my newly thrown piece as beautiful and unique.

And so, I believe, it is with raising children. They come to us as "lumps of clay," unformed and waiting to be molded. It is our job as parents to mold and fashion the clay using all of the tools we have and the tools we acquire along the way. Just like centering the clay in pottery, we as parents must remain centered with our core values and beliefs guiding us through this process. If we are "off-center" this task becomes much more difficult.

And as hard as we try to move our children in a certain direction, sometimes they won't move the way we had envisioned. As an amateur potter, I've found that clay does seem to move on its own and while we as the parents/potters may have intended a plate, a bowl will emerge. A good potter, like a good parent, is able to begin the process of movement,

---

*Translation by Reb Zalman Schachter-Shalomi, received via Rabbi Daniel Siegel

recognizing and following the movement to see what emerges. By using skill and insight, technique and intuition, something beautiful and unique always emerges.

ג

"U'vara vo nikavim nikavim chalulim chalulim. Galui v'yadua lif-nei kee-sei k'vodecha she'im y'patei'ach echad meihem or y'satem echad meihem ee efshar l'hitkayem v'la'amode l'fanecha.

...creating openings, arteries, glands, and organs, marvelous in structure, intricate in design. Should but one of them, by being blocked or opened, fail to function, it would be impossible to exist.

For those of you who have or can remember back to having young children in potty training mode, I'm sure you might recall that it was all about the pee and the poop. Running to the toilet, sitting and waiting, getting off the toilet, running back to the toilet and then finally getting accolades for making just a tiny drop in the potty. I remember seeing my two-year-old daughter standing to the left of the toilet bowl, pulling up her shirt and exposing her diaper and then leaning into the bowl and telling us that she was trying to make a pee-pee. Having watched her two older brothers, she assumed that's how everyone goes to the potty.

This *Asher Yatzar* prayer is often referred to as the bathroom prayer because one recites it after exiting the lavatory. Why would there be a prayer to recite after going to the bathroom? Well, speaking from experience, for anyone who has ever had any gastrointestinal complications, I think you understand why we need to be thankful for a human body that was "fashioned in wisdom, with openings, arteries, glands and organs, all marvelous in structure, intricate in design that work the way they should! If one of them fails to function by being blocked or opened, it would be impossible to exist." I remember my six-year-old asked me what would happen if all the poop and pee stayed inside his body and didn't come out? My response was, "Well, let's thank God that it all does come out!"

One of Judaism's basic beliefs teaches us not to take anything for granted. In fact, the Talmud instructs us to recite a minimum of 100 blessings each day.* Blessings range from the physical to the emotional, the mental, and the spiritual realms. Through our daily gratitude practice, Judaism hopes that we learn not to take things for granted.

In raising my kids, I have tried to integrate gratitude into our lives—for food, clothing, shelter, and healthy bodies. When they are sick and are stuck in bed, I talk to them about how bodies perform miracles and are made to self-heal, each part working in harmony with the others to help them get better.

While reciting a thank-you after going to the bathroom might seem like a little thing, I believe that it is reflective of a much larger concept: to practice an attitude of gratitude. As my children are way past potty training, my challenge now is to reconnect to that original excitement and amazement I felt during those years, and to remember how to appreciate the miraculous bodies we have.

ד

Baruch Atah Adonai rofeh chol basar umaflee la'asote.

Praised are You, Adonai healer of all flesh,
who sustains our bodies in wondrous ways.

I spend much of my scarce spare time reading cooking and health magazines, which have provided me with insight into the importance of eating good, clean food. It is important to me that my kids learn to take care of and respect their bodies. In an age of fast food and junk food galore, I want them to value natural foods that help their bodies grow and stay healthy. Every time they watch TV, they are inundated by ads that target their little eyes and their taste buds for products such as Trix, GoGurt, and Lucky Charms. When I do my best to find more natural alternatives,

---

*Babylonian Talmud, Menachot 43b.

The Talmud is the book of Jewish law and legends that was compiled between the years 200-500 C.E. It is also a record of conversations between the Rabbis about the details and principles of Judaic practice. By reciting one hundred *brakhot* (blessings) a day, we connect our daily experiences of life to Source.

somehow Stonyfield Farms just doesn't have the same allure as GoGurt. Every time I'm at the grocery store with one of my children, I feel under attack, "Mom, can we get this…Mom, can we get that…" Try as I may, I constantly feel like I'm fighting an uphill battle. I do my best to stay on course, and so I wage the whole wheat versus white argument with my son daily. Every single time I make pasta or a sandwich, my kids push back.

To honor my child's tenth birthday and to try to add some humor to our ongoing argument, I purchased for him a bag filled with white flour products: Wonder Bread, white spaghetti noodles, and a few other white flour goodies. I got quite a smile from that gift when he asked, "Why can't you just buy this stuff all year long?" Unexpectedly, I heard the words that I swore I would never say, "When you grow up and have a house of your own, you can buy and make whatever you'd like, but in my house, I choose to buy whole wheat products." How it drove me crazy when my parents said that to me!

Now, as a parent, I see things differently. When I say those words to my children, it's not to drive them crazy; rather, it is to encourage them to think about the choices that I make as their mother and the choices that ultimately they will have to make for themselves.

I have come to this understanding not only over many years and through much study, but also from the wisdom of the words in this prayer. When I read these words, *"Praised are You, Adonai healer of all flesh, sustaining our bodies in wondrous ways,"* I am struck by how God has created a world in which we have everything that we need to sustain ourselves. Part of that sustaining, for me, includes farming in a way that protects the soil, trees, animals, and people who inhabit our shared planet. Doing our best to grow our food free of pesticides and insecticides is part of creating a healthy food chain. I believe that we are partners with God in healing our bodies and that agricultural sustainability should be included in that partnership. Just as God fashioned our bodies in wisdom, may we, too, strive in wisdom to make good choices that in turn help our bodies and our ecosystem to function and thrive in the best way possible.

I hope I live long enough to see what food choices my children make for their children. Will it be white or wheat?

Ways to Help Stay Healthy

1) Eat a well-balanced diet.
2) Incorporate more fruits and vegetables into your diet.
3) Exercise, play outside, or join a sports team.
4) Count your blessings every day that your body is working!
(or focus on the parts of your body that do work)
5) Add whole grains to your diet.
6) Eat in moderation.
7) Get a good night's sleep.

Choices: Questions to Consider

1) Can you think of a time when you were sick, and your body was not working the way you wanted it to? How long did it take to recover? How did you feel upon recovery?
2) In what ways can you infuse the meaning of this prayer into your life?
3) How do you teach your children to take care of their bodies? How do you take care of yours?

Friendship
(V'ahavta l'reyacha kamocha)

א

*V'ahavata l'reyacha **kamocha**.*

...and you should love your neighbor **as yourself**.

What parent doesn't worry that their child won't have friends? As a parent of toddlers, I wondered—at what stage would they stop parallel playing and start talking to each other? As a parent of young children, I pondered—at what stage would they stop hitting, grabbing, and kicking one another? As a parent of elementary aged kids, I inquired—at what stage would they actually have conversations? Now, as a parent of teenagers, I wonder—at what stage will they truly look out for each other and confide in one another? As an adult, I appreciate the importance of friendship and desperately want to transmit that value to my children.

This three-word prayer taught me one of life's most important and powerful lessons. Yes, it is important to love your neighbor as yourself, however, first *you* have to love *yourself*. As a parent, I believe this is one of my most important jobs: teaching my children to love themselves. For if they do not love themselves first, how will they be able to truly love another person?

But how do we teach them to love themselves?

First and foremost, we have to love them for who they are, not for who we want them to be. Recognizing our children's strengths and gifts helps reinforce their psyche and spirit, knowing that they have innate value, gifts given to them from God. Some are lucky and uncover their talents early, while others spend much longer trying to discover them. If I can help my child uncover their special talents and qualities, I believe that I am moving them closer to loving themselves.

It was breakfast time several years ago when I overheard my son tell my daughter that she wasn't so good in math and that he was much smarter than she was. He continued repeating this idea to her in as many ways as he could articulate. Usually, I try to let my kids work things out by themselves (unless physical contact is involved) so I just listened. But after about five minutes, I couldn't hold my tongue any longer and I lost it. It was not one of my better Mommy moments.

I was speaking in a louder than normal decibel level; OK, I was yelling. "If I hear you tell your sister one more time how much smarter in math you are than she is, I am going to lose it." (The truth is, I already had!) "Each of you has special gifts from God, not to mention the fact that she is an excellent math student and enrolled in enrichment in her first grade class. Some of us are better in math, some better in reading, some talented in music, some in auto repair. The bottom line is that we are each special and each of us has something special to contribute to our world. I don't ever want to hear you telling your sister or anyone else, for that matter, that you're better than them. God created everyone in God's image, and no one is better than anyone else. Do you understand?"

Taking some deep breaths, smiling sweetly, I got off my soapbox and continued fixing breakfast. There was silence for the rest of the meal. In retrospect, I probably shouldn't have yelled; however, his words triggered something so deep in me that I was no longer able to stay silent. Later in the day, I apologized to my son for yelling, with an explanation of my irate response in the hope that he took what I said seriously.

From my experience, the idea that each of us has special, unique gifts from God is central to helping kids learn to love themselves. We are all essential pieces in God's Grand Puzzle of Life. Just as a puzzle with one missing piece won't bring completion, so, too, God's plan cannot be complete without every one of us. Perhaps using this visual with our children will encourage them to explore their uniqueness. Once they recognize their own intrinsic value, they will perceive other people's value as well. Loving others will become simply a continuation of loving themselves.

Ways to Help Kids Love Themselves

1) Experiment with different activities
so kids can see where they excel.
2) Catch them doing good deeds and
compliment them on their kindness.
3) Share with them ways and reasons you love them so much.
4) Praise them when they really deserve it,
but don't overpraise, as it loses its meaning.
5) Talk to your kids about how
you discovered what is special about you.
6) Have kids keep a journal and write down
experiences that they are proud of.

ב

V'ahavata l'reyacha kamocha.
...and you should love your neighbor as yourself.

How do we teach our children to be good friends? What exactly does it mean to love our neighbor as ourselves? For more than 1,800 years, this question has been debated in Jewish tradition. We read in the Babylonian Talmud that there was a non-Jew who wanted to convert to Judaism, so he went to see Rabbi Shammai and asked to be taught the entire Torah while standing on one foot. Scoffing, Rabbi Shammai told him it was an impossibility. Unhappy with that answer, he went to see Rabbi Hillel and asked him the same question. Unfazed, Rabbi Hillel stood on one foot and said, "What is hateful to you, do not do to another. This is the whole Torah, go and study it; the rest is commentary." The non-Jew was so impressed by Rabbi Hillel's response that he converted and went to study.* This teaching, referred to as the "Golden Rule," has been reworded throughout the ages as "Do unto others as you would have them do unto

---
*Babylonian Talmud, Shabbat 31a

you." In theory, it seems like a really simple rule, but I think I share this wisdom several times a day in my house and it still does not seem to have sunk in! Despite my frustration with repetition, I really do believe that this concept, while developmental in nature, is at the crux of empathy.

For me, another meaning hidden in this prayer *"And you shall love your neighbor as yourself"* teaches us the importance of empathy. Putting yourself in someone else's shoes is hard both as an adult and perhaps even more so as a child; nonetheless, I believe that it is one of the most essential elements of growing our children into *menschen*—decent, caring human beings.

One day, my youngest child was crying over a very difficult homework concept that she was unable to grasp. After hearing her crying, my eldest came over, sat next to her for about three minutes, patted her arms, asking her why she was crying. She could barely answer him, but she finally mustered, "I can't do my work!" He responded, "Can I help you?" "No, I don't want any help," she retorted. Slowly, he picked up her flashcards and gently coaxed her to review them. He then proceeded to sit with her and review all of her flashcards for about 20 minutes. I watched this entire conversation from the kitchen sink and marveled at his empathy. He has finally gotten it, after all of those times I thought I sounded like a broken record—he finally got it! It was so beautiful to watch one of my children taking care of another one.

Later that night, I was tucking my eldest in bed and told him how proud I was that he helped his sister out. I shared with him that I could tell by how he sat with her and comforted her that he was really feeling her sadness and frustration and that I was most proud of his display of empathy. He shared that he remembered feeling that way when he couldn't get his schoolwork done and that's why he knew how she felt. Precisely, I thought to myself; that's what this is all about—love your neighbor as yourself. Show empathy and compassion. Remember how you felt in a similar situation and then use those feelings to help make it better for somebody else.

ג

V'ahavata l'reyacha kamocha.
...and you should love **your neighbor** as yourself.

I remember being a little girl and watching Sally Struthers' commercials for *Feed the Children*. She was the spokesperson for children around the world who did not have enough to eat. I vividly remember the pictures of these kids: tears, distended bellies, flies landing on their faces. Every time these commercials appeared, I would shed my own tears. They seared such images into my heart and soul that I wanted to help by sponsoring a child. With understanding and compassion, my mother always responded the same way... yep... you guessed it! "No, but when you grow up, if you want to, you can sponsor a child." At that moment, my eight-year-old self decided that was just what I would do.

Fast forward to Hanukkah 2003, twenty-seven years later. My husband asked me what I wanted as a gift. This year, I didn't want any gifts—I wanted to sponsor a child. I'm not sure what prompted me at that time to conjure up my childhood promise; but it had been resurrected and, for my own sake, I needed to make good on my promise. Since that time, I have sponsored various children over the years.

One of my most memorable correspondences was from one girl who wrote, "My family and I thank you very much. Every morning when I get up, I remember you." I was so incredibly touched by those words. They literally brought tears to my eyes. For me, this echoed my belief that we are all connected to and responsible for one another. That is what it means to love your neighbor as yourself. Just as I take care of myself, so, too, I take care of others.

The majority of children who live in the developed world have so much. How many times have I told my kids that they should be grateful for the food they have because there are so many children who go to bed hungry each night. I've told them that they should appreciate receiving a good education because there are so many in this world who remain illiterate. Each time I utter such a statement, it feels empty, vapid. How, I wonder, how do I **really** teach them?

Using the words of this prayer helped me to come up with one idea. If we look at the Hebrew word *v'ahavta*, it begins with an *aleph* and the beginning letter of the second word is a *lamed*, *l'reyacha*. The *lamed*, pronounced here as *l'*, means "to." Translating these two words would read: and you shall love **to** your neighbor. *This preposition connects these two words. If you combine the *aleph* from the first word with the *lamed* of the second word, those letters form one of God's names, *EL*. When we show **love to** our neighbors, when we connect **to** our neighbors, I offer that God is present in that connection.

As my children mature into adults and become contributing members of society, I pray that they feel connected to and responsible for other human beings, especially those whom they might not even know. These days many schools have required community service programs, which is terrific. However, my challenge as a parent is to instill the idea of *tikkun olam* (repairing the world) into my children, not because it's a graduation requirement but because, from my perspective, it is their responsibility—as Jews and as human beings sharing the planet with 7.7 billion others.

What I also hope to impress upon my children is that our helping others should not be seen from a superior vantage point (e.g., "We" are more "civilized" than "they" are, or "We" need to "teach" them the "right" way to live in this world). Rather, we help others by learning about them and about their culture. By recognizing that we have much to learn from them, I hope that we will learn more about ourselves. We learn in *Pirkei Avot, Ethics of the Fathers,* that Rabbi Ben Zoma teaches, "Who is wise? One who learns from everyone." Teaching my children this message will help them balance the responsibility they have to help make the world a better place by not solely imposing their way of doing things. Not an easy lesson to both teach and learn; indeed it is a delicate balance to maintain.

When we recite this prayer, we can focus on the fulcrum, the connection between the *aleph* and the *lamed*. We can think about the **love** we need to show **to** our neighbor. It is almost as if there is an imaginary seesaw between the two letters. We strive for love with the aleph and strive for

---

*While the word truly begins with a vav, the vav is a connector meaning "and." The root of the word is ahv—meaning *to love*, and begins with the letter *aleph*. It is interesting to note that the word "vav" is a hook or connector and mirrors the role that the lamed plays in also seeking to connect.

respect with the lamed.

From our local neighbors to our geographically distant neighbors, through caring and connection, we fulfill the *mitzvah* (commandment) of loving our neighbors as ourselves. When we do that, I can't help but feel that God's light and presence will be felt deeply by us all.

Ways to Love Your Neighbor as Yourself

1) Read books about children and families from around the world. Discuss similarities and differences between your family and theirs.
2) Sponsor a child from another country or find a microloan for people in the developing world.
3) Sign up for a community service project as a family.
4) Contact a local organization that helps seniors and see if you can help them out by driving them to appointments or taking them to the market.
5) Donate your gently used items and have your children come with you to deliver them.
6) Have your child donate one of their birthday presents to a child less fortunate.

Friendship: Questions to Consider

1) How do you show love to your children? To your partner? To your self?
2) What are your strengths? What do you love about yourself?
3) What are your child's strengths? What do you love about your child? Ask your children what they love about themselves.
4) How can you help your child discover their strengths?
5) How can you love your neighbor as yourself?
6) How do you define neighbor? What responsibilities do you believe you have toward your neighbors?

Gratitude
(Birkot HaShachar)

א

Baruch Ahtah Adonai Eloheinu Melech HaOlam pokei'ach ivrim.

Praised are You, Adonai, Our God, Ruler of the Universe
who opens the eyes of the blind.*

The other day I was driving my daughter to school. It was a typical
morning except for the fact that she had just gotten her first pair of glasses.
She was instructed to wear them at school and, if needed, at other times
during the day. Carefully, she removed them from their case and gently
placed them on her face.

Silence.

A few seconds later I hear an exuberant, "I love the world." I waited
before responding, and then she continued, "I love the world, Mom. It is
so beautiful. Is this what everyone else sees? Wow, look at all the colors.
It's so bright. I just love it, Mom." I wasn't quite sure how to respond, but
I was sure that I had just witnessed God opening up the eyes of the blind.
Despite the fact that I felt like a horribly negligent parent for allowing her
vision to get so poor without my having noticed, I was grateful for having
witnessed her experience the world in living color.

Using my daughter's experience allows me to understand one meaning
behind this prayer. My daughter's "somewhat blind" eyes were opened to
see the beauty of the world. I will always remember the look of awe and
wonder on her face as our ordinary drive to school became extraordinary.

*This blessing and the ones that follow in this chapter are excerpted from a longer string
of blessings known as Birchot HaShachar (Blessings of the Dawn) that appear in the
beginning of the morning service. These blessings serve to remind us to be grateful for
those things in our lives that we may take for granted, some of which include the movement from night to day, the meeting of our basic needs, and pride in our Jewish heritage.
Reciting these blessings first thing in the morning helps us calibrate our mindset toward
gratitude before we prepare to go on with the rest of our day.

While thanking God for opening up the eyes of the blind can be read literally, I believe that these words can also be read figuratively. All of us are metaphorically "blind" in different situations. Some of us are "blind" to others' feelings; some of us are "blind" to new experiences; and some of us are "blind" when dealing with certain subject areas such as physics, economics, or English. Asking God to open our eyes means allowing ourselves to see things from a fresh perspective or gaining an understanding that we might not have had previously. I believe that sharing this idea with our kids can be extremely helpful, especially as they mature.

There are many things that at first try we may not succeed in, like being a good friend. It takes time to learn to read social cues, to understand facial expressions, to be patient and understanding, and to learn how and when to put others' needs before your own. Many elements are involved in being a good friend; but once this process is learned and eventually integrated into our children's psyches, they won't have to go through the "Friendship Checklist." Instead, they will know intuitively how to be a good friend because their eyes will have been opened.

Obtaining this gift of understanding, of sight, both literally and figuratively, can fill us with gratitude. Gratitude to see the beauty in our world on a daily basis, not just when we put glasses on for the first time. Gratitude for the gift of being able to obtain a new understanding, a fresh perspective that can help us navigate through relationships, situations, and ultimately, life itself.

Baruch Ahtah Adonai Eloheinu Melech HaOlam hanotein li kol tzarki.

**Praised are You, Adonai, our God, Ruler of the Universe
who provides me with all my needs.**

How often do we say we need something, when in reality we actually want something? I was reminded of this concept when my kids were studying needs and wants in first grade. They would come home and tell me, "Mom, today we learned that we only *need* food, water, shelter, and clothing." For a while after that, when I told them I needed them to brush their teeth, one of them would chirp back, "Mom, you don't *need* us to brush our teeth, you *want* us to brush our teeth." "Ok, you are technically right, but please go brush your teeth...now!" Needs and wants are so often interchanged in our everyday speech. We rarely stop to think if we need something or if we simply want it. For a few days following my first-grader's new realization, our family was careful with our words. Do we really *need* this, or do we really *want* this?

As time moved on, they too forgot this distinction and I started hearing things like, "Mom, I really need a cell phone." And it was my time to smile back, responding, "Need or want?" By this time, they were much older and started pleading their case. "Well, actually need, Mom. I mean, what if you're coming to pick me up and you don't know where I am, or if my plans change and you can't find me? I'd need a phone... and it's not just for me, it's actually beneficial for you." My, how far we've come since first grade!

In all seriousness, this discussion that began many years ago can provide a valuable springboard to discuss what we want versus what we need. Over the years, my family has had many challenging conversations about the difference between these two, and I try to the best of my ability to move the conversation to gratitude. I'm pretty sure that my kids are sick of hearing me repeat myself, but when they start whining about what they *need*—things that, in my opinion, should really fall under what they *want*— I just start saying things like, "I am so grateful that I have a home and a comfy bed and good food to eat and parents who love me and siblings to play with and a great school to attend, and..." By this point, they usually get the message and stop their whining. Sometimes, I'll get lucky and the reframing that I ("annoyingly") offer can help to refocus what really matters. The Gameboy or the Xbox that they "needed" so desperately just a few seconds ago quietly fades into the background. I know that it may be a temporary fade, and that I will have to repeat myself thousands of times before the truly important things in life move to the forefront of their brains, but I'm okay with simply planting the seeds of gratitude. All good things take time to grow.

When I read the words of this prayer, *Baruch Ahtah Adonai Eloheinu*

Melech ha'olam hanotei li kol tzarkie—Praised are you, Ruler of the Universe who provides me with all of my needs—I am reminded that God does provide us with all of our needs. The majority of you who are reading this book most likely have food, shelter, and clothing. For those we see in the world who do not have these basic necessities, I still believe that they have been provided for; the problem arises in how the resources are (or are not) distributed to others. I believe that we are all responsible to help one another secure life's basics needs. And I contend that God provides us with the capacity for faith, hope, and love so that we can reach out to help others in need.

One of my most important jobs as a Mom is to help my kids realize the difference between a "need" and a "want" and to connect them to their own capacity for faith, hope, and love.

ג

Baruch Ahtah Adonai Eloheinu Melech Ha-olam hanotein l'ayef ko'ach.

Praised are You, Adonai, our God, Ruler of the Universe
who gives strength to the weary.

I remember the fatigue, the sheer and utter exhaustion, of waking up six times a night to nurse my babies. With my first child, I truly had no idea what I was doing. Thanks to much help from an amazing lactation consultant, I learned how to nurse successfully; nonetheless, I still remember the bleary-eyed nights that seemed endless. How much longer could I survive waking up so often during the middle of the night? I tried to sweeten my fatigue by working hard to cherish those quiet times alone with my baby. I tried to rationalize my fatigue by connecting myself to women all over the world who were also awake, nursing their little ones. We shared a camaraderie that transcended time and space; yet as I tried to focus on those beautiful notions, I was just so darn tired that I didn't know how I could continue.

Eventually, the months and years of physical exhaustion that I endured in raising infants and toddlers passed, but only to be transformed into the mental exhaustion of raising elementary and middle-school aged children, and later guiding perplexing teenagers.

Baruch Ata Adonai Eloheinu Melech Ha-olam hanotein l'ayef ko'ach.

Praised are You, Ruler of the Universe who gives strength to the weary.

This prayer is one of my favorites, as I often feel the need to pray for strength. When my kids were younger, I prayed for physical strength; now that they are older, I pray for mental and emotional strength.

It was another regular day when the phone rang at 2:00 P.M. My son's English teacher was calling to discuss his poor behavior that afternoon. The two of them had been having a hard time working together and the teacher finally felt it necessary to give my son a referral, which remains on his school record. Now, granted, he was in sixth grade; but this experience, I'm sorry to say, was nothing new. I'd had frequent conversations with many administrators at my son's school, some positive, but mostly not. Each time I engaged in a conversation, I took a deep breath and tried to maintain my equanimity. Sometimes I succeeded, but many times I failed. The job of child-rearing had become exasperating!

Just when things seemed to be sailing along smoothly—wham!! There were many days and months during which I felt like a permanent inhabitant of the Land of Wham, waiting and praying for those moments of solace, glimpses of calm. I never knew what to expect or when the phone was going to ring, which I suppose was part of my great frustration. Just when I thought that things had calmed down, wham! Something else exploded. I felt like I always had to be on my toes, waiting with bated breath for the next episode of "Motherhood: The Journey of the Unknown."

After my conversation with the English teacher, I called my Mom to vent and debrief. Her response was always the same: "I don't know how you do it, Ame." And my response was also always the same: "What is my option?" There are no money-back guarantees when you have a child. And while I certainly don't want to trade mine in, there are some days when I feel broken, vanquished, defeated.

I often meditate on my Mom's remark and, after sitting quietly trying to regroup, I find myself asking God for strength—strength to continue parenting under enormous stress. I utter the words of this prayer nearly daily. I want to express my gratitude to God for giving me strength during my weariest times—those times when I don't think I have one more second of patience left, and all I want to do is go into my room and cry and scream. As a parent, I am grateful to God for blessing me with patience, even when I think that my patience has run out; blessing me with love, even when my well feels dry; and blessing me with understanding, even when my reserves have dwindled.

Praised are You, Adonai our God, Ruler of the Universe, who gives strength to the weary. Amen!

ד

Baruch Ahtah Adonai Eloheinu Melekh ha-olam mateer asurim.

**Praised are You, Adonai, our God, Ruler of the Universe
who releases the bound.**

One day, an unbelievable event occurred in my house. My kids were fighting. Now that wasn't the unbelievable part—what followed was. They were chasing each other, teasing and yelling, and finally in desperation I separated all of them, sent them to their rooms, and told everyone to take a time out (including me!). After about 20 minutes, I invited everyone to the dinner table, but my eldest decided to wait until the other two were finished before he came out of his room. After clearing his plate from the table, he looked at a piece of mail that was on the counter. It was a letter from American Jewish World Service (AJWS) and on the front was a pair of hands covered in oil. He asked what it was; I told him to read the inside. He read about the Achuar Indians and how their drinking water had become polluted by the Pluspetrol oil company of Argentina. AJWS was working with other grassroots organizations to help these indigenous people in their fight to reclaim clean water and prevent future deaths of their loved ones. He noticed a card inside asking for donations to help these people. He closed the letter, left the kitchen, and that was that.

Or so I thought.

About five minutes later, he came back to the kitchen with $15 of his saved money and told me that he wanted to send it to help the Achuar Indians. With tears in my eyes and pride in my heart, I asked him what made him want to do this? He said, "I was thinking about how mad I was before [with my siblings], and then I thought about how much madder I would be if I didn't have any water to drink and the water I had looked like this, so I decided that I wanted to help them." With that, he placed two slick five-dollar bills and five crumpled one-dollar bills in the card and filled in $15 donation on the response card.

It was as if a switch in him had been flicked. Wow, I felt like I had just witnessed an unbelievable transformation. My eleven-year-old had been bound by anger and frustration and had just been set free. I am not sure whether he had been released from his anger or simply released himself, but it didn't matter. What did matter was that he had transformed his anger into goodness and kindness. I murmured a prayer of gratitude to God for the privilege of seeing this moment.

Praised are You, Adonai, our God, Ruler of the Universe who releases the bound. When I recite this line, I think about my son and how he was released from his anger, how he moved from negativity to positivity. I believe that this ability to move from negative emotions to positive emotions is a value that can help our children grow into healthy adults. Sometimes we can learn from our children and sometimes they can learn from us.

As difficult as it may be for us as parents, I hope that we can serve as role models for our kids. Knowing that we, as adults, will be bound up by many life challenges and powerful emotions, we can choose to show our children how we work to free ourselves from what binds us. We can share our experiences and emotions with them and walk them through our own inner process, as we move to release ourselves from our bonds. After such a sharing, perhaps our children would be open to redirecting their own anger, focusing on the goodness that is in their lives. This releasing process is not easy and won't happen overnight,* but in the meantime, if we are able to gently nudge our children when we see them

---

*Please remember that children must be at the developmentally appropriate age before they are able to be introspective. I would suggest not trying with children younger than 10, but each child's maturity is different. Trust your gut.

bound by envy, anger, jealousy, frustration, or greed, we can point out to them that their greatness is being compromised. Just as we say to God, *Praised are You who releases the bound*, so too can we, as parents, teach our children to release what binds them. With this releasing comes a large amount of gratitude. When we are able to free ourselves or be freed from those times and emotions that bind us, we may find ourselves overcome with appreciation for a newfound sense of freedom that now occupies our bodies, our minds, and our souls.

Ways to Promote Gratitude

1) Notice the sunrise and/or the sunset each day.
2) Say a quick blessing over food. There are traditional blessings, or you can create your own, such as "Thank you God for this yummy food."
3) Go through old toys and clothes on a regular basis and donate them. Talk about how much we each *need* versus how much we *want*.
4) Only under adult supervision:
Tie each other's hands with a rope.
Stay tied up for one minute.
Release the rope and talk about how it felt to be tied up versus released. Try to find an emotional situation that mirrored this physical example of feeling/being "bound up" and discuss what can free us up psychologically.
5) Before bedtime, share three things you experienced during the day for which you're grateful.

Gratitude: Questions to Consider

1. How do you "see" the world? Are there things that blind you?
2. Why is it easier for others to see what sometimes blinds us? How can we receive this insight and help ourselves to "see" more clearly?
3. Discuss *needs* versus *wants*. How might you use that knowledge for future challenging situations?

Words Matter

(Baruch She'amar)

א

Baruch She'amar v'haya ha'olam.

Praised is God whose word created the world.

There are moments in one's life when we are deeply affected by what at the time seems to be a miniscule event; however, it settles in your psyche and remains until it is ready to be reexamined. To this day, decades later, I still hold the memory of seeing the movie *Mommie Dearest* as a seventh grader. I was shocked to see that there were mommies who treated their children the way that little girl was treated. Remaining in the movie theater was actually quite painful for me. In reflecting back to that time, I guess I made a silent pact with myself that when I became a mom, I would never, ever treat or talk to my children in the abusive way that Joan Crawford spoke to her daughter Christina.

Actions and words have power and our tradition understands that in a very deep way. Just look at how the world was created in the book of Genesis... with words: "And God said, 'Let there be light,' and there was light... God said, 'Let there be an expanse...' and God said, 'Let there be vegetation...'" Each time God speaks, another aspect of creation unfolds.* God speaks the world into being, bit by bit. In the *Baruch She'amar* prayer, this creation of the world with words is referenced again, which made me think about the incredible power of our words. When we speak to our children, we create their worlds and their worldview. If we want to create loving, confident, compassionate children then we, too, must choose our words very carefully.

From this prayer, I learned that we create our reality based on how we think and how we speak. When we think positive, happy thoughts,

---

*Genesis, chapter 1

our lives become a reflection of that positivity and happiness; when we think negative, unpleasant thoughts, our lives become a reflection of this negativity. It took me a while to realize how, as parents, we have such a tremendous impact on how we help our children develop.

I remember the first time one of my children accidentally spilled his cup of milk. Gently, I told him not to worry and asked him to please get a towel to clean it up. I added that I'm sure it was just an accident. (Insert flashbacks to *Mommie Dearest* here.) I could have yelled, "What happened?" or "How could you be so careless?" or "Pay more attention next time!" but I knew that this kind of response would not serve to bolster my child's confidence or self-esteem. Of course, I don't always succeed in responding with this level of patience, but I try very hard to stay centered during these moments and to carefully guard my words.

An eighteenth-century German rabbi, Rabbi Akiba Eiger, was also mindful of the power of words and the effect they can have on others. He was known for regularly inviting guests to his Passover seder. One year while he was leading a large seder, a guest knocked over his cup of wine on the beautiful white tablecloth. Wanting to prevent his guest from feeling embarrassed, the rabbi himself bumped the table and spilled his own wine glass, exclaiming, "Oh, this table must be off balance!"* What a great way to avoid humiliating his guest; what a wonderful way to use his words. Whenever someone in my house spills something (including me!), I think back to that story and use it as my spilling mantra.

OK, so now you might be thinking, what difference does it make if I lose my cool when my kid spills some milk? What's the big deal if I lose my temper? Nothing, if it happens occasionally; it shows that we're human. But when we start to yell at our kids for little things they do, the little things add up. And when we continue to yell, those negative thoughts and words gradually affect our children's sense of self. Those negative thoughts and words become imprinted in our children's psyches and souls. They may begin to see themselves as clumsy, or worthless, or helpless, or no good. It might seem like a big leap, going from spilling a bit of milk to imprinting a lack of self-esteem, but building our children's confidence

---

A Different Night, Noam Zion and David Dishon. Jerusalem: The Shalom Hartman Institute, 1997, 25.

does not happen by simply turning on the "Activate Child Confidence" switch; it happens over days and months and years. It happens when we give them unconditional love and teach them with kind words how to grow into responsible and capable adults.

Ways to Help Shape Our Children's Worlds for the Better

1) Think before you speak.
2) Phrase things using "I" language (i.e., "I would appreciate it if you could please clean up your room" or "I like when things are neat" vs. "You keep your room so messy; clean it up").
3) Try to compliment your child at least three times a day when they help around the house.
4) "Catch" your child doing an act of kindness and let him/her know about it.
5) When you're frustrated, try to phrase things with positive language over negative language. ("Can you please come help take the garbage out?" vs. "How can you live in such a dump?")

ב

Baruch omer v'oseh. Baruch gozer u'mikayem.

Blessed is God who says and does.
Blessed be God who decrees and fulfills the decree.

I think one of the most challenging things about being a parent is keeping my word. I say so many things over the course of a day that it is sometimes impossible to remember what I said and to whom I said it. "That's it, if you choose not to brush your teeth tonight, then there will be no sweets tomorrow"; or, "OK, if you don't stop teasing your brother, I'll take 15 minutes off your computer time." And then the next day passes and I realize that I forgot to uphold the said consequence. And what am I supposed to do? How great would it be if consequences worked retroactively? Does it still count if the consequence is upheld a day late? Over the years and many missed consequences, I've learned that whenever possible I should give immediate consequences—that way I'm more likely to remember what I said.

I think back to when my first child was two-and-a-half years old. We were at an open gym having a great time, and then he went over to another child and hit her. The first time he hit, I explained very kindly that we don't hit, that it hurts the other child, and that it's not nice. The second time he hit her, I told him that I had already told him once and that if I saw him hit her again, I would take him home. The third time he hit her, I swooped him up and explained to him that I had already told him twice; we were leaving. I took him outside and we put his shoes back on. As he watched the other kids playing and having fun I reminded him why we were leaving and told him that next week we could come back to try again, as long as he remembered that hitting was not allowed.

While I might have seemed sure in my actions, internally, I was wondering if this event would scar my child. Was I being too harsh? After all, he was only two-and-a-half. Was I making the right decision? Despite this self-talk, I finished putting on my son's shoes and was about to leave when the gym teacher came over to me and told me how impressed she was to see that I was keeping my word.

As a first-time Mom who often questioned my decisions, it was reassuring to hear this from a veteran teacher of thirty years. She continued by telling me, "I can't tell you how many times I have heard parents make empty threats. If you're not going to remove your kid from the class, don't say that you're going to! Anyway, keep up the good work; it'll pay off later." Although I didn't quite get the "it'll pay off later" part, I felt good that I had said what I meant and meant what I said. I believe that sometimes God places messengers in our path to reassure us that we're doing the right thing. I am forever grateful to Miss Carol for helping me feel confident during a moment of great uncertainty.

Ten years and two kids later, I get what she meant. Now, my children know that if I say something, I mean it. If I give them consequences,

I've learned to follow through. Sometimes, it's hard—really, really hard. Especially when I go a bit overboard, like telling my eight-year-old he was grounded for a month for throwing a book at his brother's face. Yeah, it was a really solid throw - but a month, a whole month?! As the words came out of my mouth, I was wishing that I could eat them and change the consequence to maybe two weeks; but it was too late, and so I did follow through. But I made a note to self to think before I speak.

When I read *Baruch omer v'oseh. Baruch gozer um'kayem*, it is a reminder for me that just as God says and does and decrees and fulfills the decree, we too must keep our words and do what we say we are going to do. Kids are smart, and they know if we'll keep our words or if we are pushovers. By keeping our words, we show our children that we are people of integrity and that we uphold our word. Words matter, and by teaching our children this, we are implicitly teaching them that what they say also matters. Having integrity, being truthful, and following through are three qualities that I learned from *Baruch She'amar.*

Ways to Keep Our Words

1) Think before you shout out your consequence.
2) Prepare yourself for times when you think you may lose your cool by having one-liners ready
(e.g., "I need to think about that" or
"Let me get back to you before I give you my answer").
3) Follow through on what you say.
4) Talk with your kids about the power of words.
5) Empower your kids to use their words to express how they are feeling and then validate their experience of doing so.

ג

Baruch miracheim al ha'aretz. Baruch miracheim al habriyot.

God has compassion for the land.
God has compassion for all of God's creatures.

"To squash or not to squash?" that is my eternal question. When I see a bug in my house, do I kill it or not? What about a lizard? Does the size of the bug determine whether I'm going to remove it from my house? Do I kill the bugs even if the kids are watching? There are so many millions of ants in this world; does it really matter if I take out a few? Well, after twenty years of living in tropical Florida, I have reached a compromise. I have come to terms with killing little bugs, but the big spiders and lizards I take outside. Nonetheless, I still feel guilty about killing those littlest of critters, especially if my children catch me doing so.

How do I teach my children to have compassion for the land and for God's creatures? My first but not so totally honest step is to eliminate the ants while no one is watching. Despite these ant removals, I have tried to teach my kids to be grateful and respectful for all of God's creatures. As young as toddlers, we would talk about being kind and gentle to animals. I remember when I saw one of my toddlers poking at a lizard, I quickly let him know that we are not allowed to be unkind to animals. In fact, just the opposite, we have a responsibility to take care of them.

Outdoor play was encouraged on a daily basis and on most days they would catch bugs and worms, play in the mud, dig and "garden." Each day was a fight to see who would be the one to water the plants. They would run and scream when we would find our "pet" snake slithering in our yard. They enjoyed the adorable baby birds we found nesting in our bougainvillea plant. They would run away and hide when the mama bird swooped down to be sure her babies were protected. At the beach, they collected seashells and saved them in their treasure boxes. At every opportunity, I encouraged my children to love and respect nature.

Today, it's become hip to be "eco-friendly" and "green." There is even a new movement called "eco-kashrut," * but this idea of taking care of the world began thousands of years ago with the Torah.** I support each of these endeavors to help make our world more sustainable and I believe that one of my jobs as a parent is to raise my children's consciousness about our home planet, Earth.

To that end, I am always looking for new ideas to help them feel connected and responsible for our planet. When we shop, we bring reusable bags. We donate *tzedakah* to plant trees and work locally to plant vegetation. We have an herb and vegetable garden. Showers are (supposed to be) limited to five minutes, which has gotten harder as my children have gotten older. Water is (supposed to be) turned off while brushing teeth. I've tried to help my children understand that our natural resources are limited and that we are all responsible to take care of Mother Earth.

When I read "*Baruch miracheim al ha'aretz. Baruch miracheim al habriot.* God has compassion for the land. God has compassion for all of God's creatures," I know that my job is ongoing. As a mom striving to act in God's image, I want to teach and model compassion for the land and for all creatures. I think I may have to rethink the whole killing bugs thing.

---

* This idea of eco-kashrut was introduced in recent decades, most notably by Rabbi Zalman Shachter Shalomi, founder of the Jewish Renewal movement, who believed in incorporating environmental concerns into the Jewish dietary laws.
** *Tzar ba'aley chayim*, being kind to animals, is an important Jewish value that we learn about in the Torah. One example we are taught about is not to plow with an ox and a mule together because they work at different speeds. (Deuteronomy 21:10). Another example is if you see your fellow's donkey or ox fallen on the road, you can't ignore it; you must help lift him up. (Deuteronomy 22:4)

Ways to Teach Compassion for the Land and for all of God's Creatures

1) Be kind and gentle with the land and with all creatures.
2) Adopt a pet from a local animal shelter.
3) Volunteer to do an environmental cleanup
(forest, beach, park, etc.).
4) Purchase energy-saving appliances.
5) Don't let water run unnecessarily
(when doing dishes, brushing teeth).
6) Plant trees in your yard or your neighborhood.
7) Put up a bird feeder or plant a butterfly garden.

Words Matter: Questions to Consider

1) What tone of voice do you use when you speak?
2) Have you given consequences that you regretted?
If so, how can you try to choose your words more carefully?
3) How do you work to build your child's
confidence through your words?
4) How can you identify your "triggers" so that you respond
in the most compassionate way possible at those times?

Joy

(Halleluyah)

א

Halleluyah
Let us praise God!

I remember when my now sixteen-year-old was six months old. Each morning I would walk into his room, and the second he heard the door creak open he would start to coo loudly and frantically wave his arms and hands, smiling from ear to ear. To date, it is one of my most cherished Mommy memories. What an amazing feeling for someone to be THAT happy to be awake and to see me. Of course, he knew that it was breakfast time, so I won't take all of the credit. That being said, I was and continue to be enamored with his *joie de vivre*, his zest for life.

Ever since he was a baby, he has expressed such a joy in being alive. As an infant, he loved to roll around on our down comforter, moving from side to side and just giggling. On our daily walks, he would stop and watch the squirrels jump onto the trees and just start to squeal with delight. How wonderful to see the world with those eyes, to see the world anew each day.

My experience has been that most kids see the world that way, with grand excitement as they splash in puddles, mix water and dirt to make really cool mud cakes, and wander outside in nature to notice what many of us grown-ups just walk past. As adults we have become jaded. We step on bugs and crush little flowers that we affectionately call weeds; we avoid puddles and certainly don't spend our time making mud cakes, as we rush to and from work or to and from errands. If we do decide to encourage our children, some of us may set accompanying guidelines. We may let them collect bugs (if we are brave), make mud cakes (as long as they stay outside), pick the "flowers,"(checking to be sure they are really weeds and not from our neighbor's garden) and splash in puddles (with boots and raingear). Each uninhibited desire of our children often becomes tempered by our schedules and level of need for control. We may allow our children to explore and enjoy, provided that it fits with our schedule and within our self-imposed guidelines.

While this book is about how **we** can become better parents, I believe deeply that we become better parents by learning from our children. Parenting is about guiding and teaching our children, but it is also about seeing our children as mirrors. They reflect back to us what it is we need to learn. One of the most important lessons that I have learned from my children is to let go—let go of my schedules and expectations. From them I have learned that I often need to relinquish my self-imposed guidelines and ways of doing things so that I can join in the joy of my children.

Children provide us with the magical opportunity to learn to re-appreciate the small joys in life that we, as adults, tend to overlook. We can learn from our kids this great message of seeing the world anew each day and finding joy in the little things.

ב

Halleluhu b'tayka shofar
Halleluhu b'nevel v'khinor
Halleluhu b'tof u'machol
Halleluhu b'minim v'ugav

Praise God with trumpet calls.
With harp and lute praise God.
Praise God with drums and dance.
With flute and strings praise God.

When my oldest was born and I was trying to figure out how to keep him occupied during the long days, I signed him up for a Mommy and Me music class. There was something about shaking the maracas and tambourines, clapping the castanets, and "singing" into the fake microphone that he loved. Each week he looked forward to going to this music class. I made a note to self and tucked his love for music away. Many years later, when he turned seven, we decided to sign him up for guitar lessons. The first few months were great as he learned finger placement and a few notes. He was able to play some short songs and we were encouraged by his progress. Then, he hit a wall and the complaining began. "I don't like guitar anymore. I don't want to practice; it's boring, and we don't do anything fun."

After speaking to his teacher, my husband and I were told that he had plateaued at his current level and that in order to move ahead, he needed to be practicing more and taking his instruction a bit more seriously. After discussing it, we decided that it would be in his best interest to continue practicing (against his will). We held our ground and "forced" him to practice. After several months, he slowly began to turn the corner; he learned some new techniques, and some new songs that he wanted to learn, and stopped complaining as frequently.

After nearly a year, we were finally able to stop nagging him completely. Soon, he began practicing on his own, without prodding. Interestingly, we started noticing how he would go into his room to play guitar when he was frustrated or sad or angry. It was amazing how he understood this intuitively. As the years progressed, he added electric guitar to his repertoire and then began spending several hours a day practicing. He had become passionate, dare I say obsessed, about his guitar playing. There was something about music that touched his soul. I think back to his initial Mommy and Me music class and smile when I think about how music has always spoken to him. Now, as a teenager, music is how he experiences the world.

One of the most challenging aspects about being a parent is knowing when to push and when to let up. Unfortunately, there are no hard and fast rules and mistakes are often made. I have learned to listen to my gut, or as I like to call it, my internal GPS, to determine where I am in a specific situation. While I have made my fair share of mistakes along the way, I find that when I listen to my inner voice, I tend to make fewer. This time with my son's guitar experience, there was an intuitive knowing that kept us nudging him and prodding him. I feel lucky and grateful that we listened.

After seeing my son's response to music, I began to think more carefully about the overall importance of the arts to all of us. My other son loves both visual arts and drama, and my daughter loves painting and photography. I once read, "If you have no art, your soul has no voice." And the older I get, the more it rings true.

By having art in their lives, my children have been able to find expression for their innermost desires and passions. They have a positive outlet to channel their emotions, their sorrows, and their joys. Whatever the art form—playing music, listening to music, singing, dancing, or drawing—all of them are ways to connect to one's soul and ultimately to God. Through the arts, we allow our children to tap into the depth of their souls, giving them the time to focus on something that brings them inner peace, happiness, and fulfillment.

From this Halleluyah prayer, we learn about the importance of music, and I would expand it to all of the creative arts. By engaging in various art forms, we show our appreciation for life—the use of our ears, our eyes, and our hands to create. Through our senses, we praise God by bringing more beauty into the world.

We read in *Bereshit* that God created the world, and yet, we work as partners with God in creation. Just as we turn wheat into bread and herbs into medicines, by creating through the arts, we become partners with God in helping to beautify the world. We praise God through sounds and strings and drums and dance. We praise God through paint and embroidery, through clay and glass, through movement and sound. Through our own creation, we enhance what God has created.

Halleluhu b'tayka shofar
Halleluhu b'nevel v'khinor
Halleluhu b'tof u'machol
Halleluhu b'minim v'ugav

Praise God with trumpet calls.
With harp and lute praise God.
Praise God with drums and dance,
With flute and strings praise God.

Ways to Experience Joy

1) Learn how to play a musical instrument.
2) Listen to music, alone or together.
3) Dance!
4) Try a new art form.
5) Go see live theater.
6) Attend a concert.
7) Enjoy the little things in life:
Jump in a puddle, make some mud cakes, pick flowers.

Joy: Questions to Consider

1) What brings you joy?
2) How much joy do you feel you have in your life?
3) How do you feel being in nature?
4) Is joy an innate character trait or can it be taught?
5) Does the level of joy you feel as an adult match
the level of joy you felt as a child? If not, what
do you think has led to that discrepancy?
6) Discuss what brings joy to your family,
as individuals and as a unit.

ג

Kol hanishama t'hallel Yah
Let every living being praise God.

One evening when my middle child was about three years old, we were driving home together. The sun was setting, and the sky was exquisite shades of pink, purple, orange, and yellow. Having lived in South Florida for nearly two decades, one of its most incredible gifts, in my opinion, is its sunsets. I desperately miss the change of seasons, the hues of the leaves in fall, the quiet of the snow in winter, the new buds poking their heads out in spring, and the levity of summer. When I first moved down here, I bemoaned the lack of seasons. In spite of missing this strong connection to nature, I have learned to find other local natural wonders such as our beaches, the Everglades, constant greenery, and magical Florida sunsets.

That evening with my toddler happened to be one of those magical nights. I glanced at my rear view mirror and saw my son with his little finger pointing to the sky and then, out of the blue, he yelled out in great excitement, "Mom, it's pink and it's pink and it's pink and it's purple and God made it just for me!"

OMG! Wow, I couldn't believe what I had just heard. Did he really just say that?

That memory will forever be seared into my consciousness on so many levels. Yes, I know that kids believe that they are the center of the universe and that life does indeed revolve around them. OK, I get that, but his words felt so much deeper. I felt as if my son was gifting me with this insight: If God made it just for him, then God made it just for me as well, and that consequently, God made it for each one of us.

Kol ha'neshama t'hallel Yah—Let all living creatures praise God. This was what my three-year-old taught his thirty-something mother on that beautiful night.

Taking note of the sunset became a metaphor for me. I was so busy raising my kids, making sure their needs were being met—physically, emotionally, intellectually, socially—that I often forgot to look up—literally and metaphorically—at the big picture. I had forgotten to praise God for all that is good and beautiful in my world. Each day I had been given opportunities to praise God: for my children, my surroundings, my health, my relationships, my work, and my play.

I am eternally grateful to my son for reminding me to praise God daily.

Respect
(Barchu)

א

Barchu et Adonai hah-m'vorahch
Baruch Adonai hah-m'vorahch l'olahm vah'ed

Praise Adonai to whom all praise is due.
Praised be Adonai who is to be praised forever and ever.

I was standing in synagogue one Shabbat morning when two couples
were celebrating anniversaries. One couple was celebrating 58 years together and the other 55. Another congregant remarked, "Wow, I'm standing between 113 years of marriage." The rabbi asked one of the women
the secret to their longevity. At first, she didn't answer, but after a few
moments she replied, "You learn to keep your mouth shut."

Listening carefully to her advice, I began to ponder the deeper message
behind her half-joking words.

What I believe she was saying was that after 58 years of being married,
the success of their relationship was based in large part on "respect." Respect the other person's right to occasionally get the last word in. Respect
the other person's ability to disagree. Respect yourself and your husband.
Once you have been in a relationship for *that* long, you realize that it is not
always important to be right; it is more important to respect your partner,
even if you don't understand why they are doing what they are doing.
Respect is earned over time, based on the relationship that has been built.

When we chant the *Barchu* prayer, "Let us praise God to whom all praise
is due," we show our respect for God, parent *par excellence*, by bowing at
the recitation of these words. We bend our knees when we recite the word
barchu and then stand up before the word "Adonai." Through the bending
of our bodies and through the language of praise, we show respect toward
God. Just as there are times in marriage when we don't understand the

ways of our spouse, there are times when we do not understand God's ways. There will be times when we want to question God and ask why things happen. Why did I lose my job? Why was I diagnosed with this illness? Why am I struggling with my kids? There will always be countless whys, but when we come to this prayer, even with all of the craziness and unknowns in our lives, we bow and offer respect to God, to *Adonai hamevorach*, the God who is blessed... even when we don't understand all the whys of our lives.

I'd like to suggest that the relationship between us and God can be seen in the relationship between us and our children. There have been many times when my children have not understood my ways and asked many questions—why do I have to do that? How come you're making me do my homework now? Why won't you buy me an iPod? Can I use my own money? Why do I have to eat those gross vegetables? Why do I have to listen to you anyway? But at the end of the day, I believe that it is important for children to show respect for their parents. Metaphorically speaking, there are times when our children have to "bow" and follow our wishes, even if they don't understand why.

However, I also believe that this respect is a two-way street. In order to have a healthy relationship, it is crucial that we respect our children. My belief is that a foundation of mutual respect should undergird a parent-child relationship. While we might not understand our children's every desire, likes or dislikes, we can work to understand and learn to respect them. Unfortunately, I learned this the hard way by determining which battles were worth fighting. Let's start with fashion. There are many clothes that my daughter loves, and I find completely unattractive, but I've learned to keep my mouth shut. We have worked out an agreement that when we go shopping together, we both have to like the clothing. We have developed a shopping relationship based on mutual respect. Of course, there are times when I feel compelled to use my veto power, but for the most part, since we worked out our rules of engagement, it happens quite infrequently.

I have also come to respect my children's food likes and dislikes. I remember reading when they were toddlers that it takes fifteen tastes before one's palette can grow accustomed to a new food. So that was my game plan—if after fifteen tries they still did not like what I was offering, they no longer had to eat it. It still drives me crazy that my kids don't eat as many vegetables as I'd like and that they are hesitant to try new food combinations, but I am working hard to respect who they are and who they are becoming as individuals.

Clothing and food likes and dislikes pale in comparison to philosophical, ideological, and theological discussions I've had with my teens. I have been told things that make my skin crawl: "I don't believe in God. All people who live in (fill in the blank) are violent. Why don't homeless people get jobs and stop begging for money? President X is bad for our country," and the list goes on. It is extremely hard during those times to hold my tongue and keep my mouth shut.* It is painstaking to show my children respect when I neither agree with nor respect their words. And yet, I truly believe that by respecting them as individuals, I will ultimately enhance the respect they have for our relationship and for me as their parent. I've come to understand that respect must move in both directions if it is going to be based in love and admiration.

My job of child-rearing has been long and arduous, covered in tears, and yes, sprinkled with laughter. We read in the Psalms, "Those who sow in tears, will reap with joy."** Perhaps it is my own desire that imagines the psalmist referring to child-rearing. Those who toil in raising their children, who devote the time, who work at the relationship despite the tears and turmoil, the disagreements and discrepancies, will ultimately reap the benefits of a joyful and loving relationship. A relationship built over time and based on mutual respect.

---

* While I do let them share their thoughts and opinions, I will not refrain from sharing information or experience as a way to counter their arguments. While healthy dialogue is encouraged, sometimes we agree to disagree.
** Psalms 126:5

ב

Barchu et Adonai hah-m'vorahch
Baruch Adonai hah-m'vorahch l'olahm vah'ed

Praise Adonai to whom all praise is due.
Praised be Adonai who is to be praised forever and ever.

One day my parents decided to take my four-year-old to the movies. As they were discussing the choice of movies, he blurted out to my mom, "Safta (Grandma), is the movie appropriate for me?" My mom told me that she tried not to burst out laughing because most four-year-olds don't usually ask such questions. She wondered where he had heard this phrase... and then it quickly occurred to her that he had probably learned it from his parents. He was simply mirroring back the language that my husband and I used with him. It is this mirroring that is found in the *Barchu* prayer. If you look at the language in this prayer, the two lines mirror each other:

Barchu *et* **Adonai** *hah-m'vorahch*
Baruch **Adonai** *hah-m'vorahch l'olahm vah'ed*

Praised is **Adonai**, to whom all **praise** is due.
Praised be **Adonai** who is to be **praised** forever and ever.

Each line has three of the same words. The first word in each line, *barchu* and *baruch*, have the same three root letters: B R CH, *bet, resh, chaf*. Then, the words *Adonai* and *hamevorach* appear in each line. There are a few extra words that aren't mirrored directly but take on similar connotations. The word *"et"* in the first line is grammatically a word that is not translated but indicates a direct object. The Rabbis interpreted this word *"et"* as a symbol of the entire alphabet, from the first letter, *aleph* to the last letter, *tav* (Both of these letters make up the word *et*). In English we say from A to Z. The word *"et"* has come to mean "everything—from beginning to end." And so it is with my experience of child-rearing. My children see, watch, and observe *all* that I do, from A to Z—the things that I do knowingly and the things I do unknowingly. My kids notice when I bite my nails, when I casually throw an apple core out my car window, when I kill a bug, and when I help a friend. They see it all, and I have come to see that it is ultimately what they mirror.

The extra words in the second line, *l'olam va'ed*, are translated as "forever." And so, from this prayer we can see that what happens in line one, happens in line two... forever. As parents we are line one; what we do and how we act and interact with our partners, our family members, our friends, our co-workers, and our neighbors will be mirrored in line two, by our children, and so on in perpetuity.

OK, so now you might be thinking, whoa... that sounds like way too much pressure. Fortunately, our Jewish tradition teaches that it is not the parents alone who create a child. We read in the Talmud, "There are three partners in creation: the Holy Blessed One, the father and the mother." When a person honors his father and her mother, God says, "It is as though I had dwelt among them and they had honored me."* It is not just the parents that make a human being, but God as well.

While the Talmud speaks to the three partners in the creation of a child, Judaism expands this understanding and shares that it is not just the parents and God who are responsible for raising a child. All of us in the Jewish community—from rabbis, cantors, educators, youth group leaders, fellow congregants, and camp counselors to extended family members and friends—are needed to help raise our children.

There is a Jewish teaching that "the people of Israel are similar to a ship. If there is a hole in the lower hold, one does not say, 'Only the lower hold has a hole in it.' Rather they must immediately recognize that the ship is liable to sink and that they must repair the hold down below."** As a community, we look after one another. If there is trouble in one area of the boat, we all need to work together to fix it. And so it is with children, as well. "It takes a village" is not just a cliché. From my personal experience, it is the truth. We need one another for support, for carpooling, for open ears, hands and hearts, and for love and strength during times of

*Babylonian Talmud, Kiddushin 30b
**Tanna De Bei Eliyahu Rabbah, Chapter 11

joy and times of challenges.

With the help of our community and to the best of our abilities, we as parents strive to help raise our children by attending to their physical, emotional, social, psychological, mental, and spiritual well-being. As they grow and we see that our children have tapped into their potential and are moving toward adulthood, we can reap the joy of being blessed by them. Ultimately, we become blessed through our children blessing us.

Just as the text says, *barchu:* Let us bless. Let us bless our children with the best parts of ourselves—with kindness and compassion, with intelligence and wisdom, with love and understanding. Let us partner with God so that they can learn to mirror the best parts of us. And once we have accomplished this, then we will be blessed—*hamevorach*—by our children becoming a blessing to us. The one who blesses (*barchu*) becomes the one who is blessed (*hamevorach*).

ג

Baruch ahtah Adonai Eloheinu melech hah-olahm,
yotseir or uvorei choshech, oseh shalom uvorei et hah-kol.

Praised are You, Adonai our God, ruler of the world
Forming light, creating darkness, making peace, creating all.

It was always with trepidation that I entered my 14½-year-old daughter's room. Knocking hesitantly, I waited for a response, not knowing if I'd be graciously "allowed" in or blatantly unwelcomed. Her moods could sway from happy-go-lucky to, shall we say, unkind beyond belief. And so one day when she called me into her room, I was quite surprised. I entered her room only to find her buried in her blankets on her bed, "Mom, come here."

I walked in and stood by her bed, listening to what she had to say, careful not to answer for fear of being kicked out. When she was done talking, I turned to walk out. As I was about to exit, I heard, "Mom, come here!"

"I am here."

"No, I mean come here, on my bed."

Now that was an unusual request. I am very, very, very rarely allowed onto that sacred space. Unsure of what to do, as I anticipated what would come next, I gingerly, climbed onto her bed.

"Mom, lay down!"

Okay, I thought to myself. I was really unsure where this was going. Preparing myself for rejection, I laid on her bed next to her and put my hand on her back.

"Don't touch me! I said just lay next to me," she exclaimed.

Smiling, I looked at her and replied, "It must be really hard to love someone and hate someone so much at the same time."

A smile emerged from her lips with a whisper, "It is."

"Do you want to talk about how hard it is to love and hate someone simultaneously? Mom come here, Mom go out, Mom, no come back. No, stay but don't touch me. What do you want me to do?" I inquired.

Trying to configure my body to lie next to her without touching was becoming more challenging. As I rested my feet on her pillow, I heard, "Please don't put your feet on my pillow."

OY! Now contorting my body, I am trying to lie next to my beautiful, moody daughter, without having my feet touch her. Suddenly, she grabs my feet and places them over hers, only to explain that I can rest my feet on top of the blanket covering her feet.

The two of us begin laughing at the insanity of this exchange and all I can think of is how much I love my crazy, hormone-raging daughter. I remember back to my own teenage days of being a young girl filled with so many emotions. My intuition told me that I needed to make some physical contact with her, and so I asked her if I could try to help alleviate some stress by giving her a back massage.

A long pause ensues, followed by a muttering of "Okay."

For the next ten minutes, I massage her tired muscles and we actually have a conversation, about little things - school, friends, stress management—and slowly I can hear and feel her start to relax. I share with her how I manage my own stress, and there is laughter. And just for a few minutes, it is just like it used to be between us.

This teenage thing has been really hard for me. Even though I had been forewarned by friends, I did not expect such intensity of emotions, on my daughter's part or mine. Intellectually, I get it; she needs to individuate, and become her own person. And yet emotionally it feels as though a dagger has been thrust into my heart. These rare moments of bonding renewed me with hope and helped me remember that our relationship is essentially one coin with two sides—light and darkness—ease and difficulty.

Praised are You, Yah, A Fountain of Blessings,
who fashions light and creates darkness, ordains the order of all creation.

The words of this prayer speak differently to me these days. Often, I feel like our relationship is filled with more darkness than light; but then there are moments that remind me to flip the coin, to realize that you can "love and hate someone at the same time." I understand. It's complicated, and it's all part of the order of creation.

The Hebrew verbs used in this phrase, *yatzar* and *bara*, connote different ways to create: creation from something (*yatzar*) and creation from nothing (*bara*). For example, when a potter fashions a jug—the root verb *yatzar* is used. The clay already existed, but the potter works with, massages, and brings to life a new creation. So, too, are our relationships fashioned, over many moments, days, and years. The individuals in a relationship already exist, and when they spend time together, sharing positive experiences, they have the potential to bring forth, to create, *yatzar*, a (*ohr*) light-filled relationship.

And then there are instances when *bara* is used. Interestingly, Jewish tradition teaches that this verb is reserved for God alone. God is the only one who can create something out of nothing. But I guess God hasn't met my teenage daughter, because when she came back from summer camp I could swear that something (chaos) had been created out of nothing (calm). All was good and sweet and wonderful before she left and then, upon her return, *voila!* Who had absconded with my sweet daughter? Yes, I know. It appeared to come out of nowhere, but it's actually been years in the making. She is on her path toward independence and part of that process means separating from her parents, especially her mother, but ouch, is it painful!

...yotseir or uvorei choshech, oseh shalom, uvorei et hah-kol.

While I was in the midst of this unsettledness, this rollercoaster ride - not knowing whether on a particular day I would be spoken to or ignored - somehow, deep down, I knew that it was going to be alright. On those rare occasions when I catch a glimpse of universal wisdom, I am graced with an arc of development, a moving from childhood... to adolescence... and finally toward adulthood.

After we praise the Holy One for fashioning light and creating darkness, we add the phrases, *oseh shalom u'vorei et ha-kol*, the maker of peace and the one who creates all. These words come from the book of Isaiah, and the Rabbis did some fascinating refashioning. The original verse reads:

"yotzer ohr u'vorei choshech, oseh shalom u'vorei rah..."

I form the light, and create darkness;
I make peace, and create evil;
I am the Lord, that does all these things.

Hmmm...now that's interesting. The language in the Bible says, "the one who makes peace and creates *rah*-most often translated as evil.* However, if we look at the context of this word, we may come up with another understanding. Just as God creates light (*ohr*) and darkness (*choshech*), so too does God create peace (*shalom*) and *rah*, or the opposite of peace. If peace, *shalom*, is wholeness, then *rah* could indicate a sense of brokenness, an absence of wholeness.** God creates all of it, which leaves us pondering, "How can God be the Source for both good and bad?" Perhaps this challenging theology was changed to read "the one who creates all" as a way to provide a softer entry point for those praying.

When we recite these words, we praise the Source of Life for the light and the darkness in our universe, for the night sky, the luminaries, and the darkness. We praise for peace and for lack of peace, for wholeness and for brokenness. As difficult as it may be, if we as parents can learn to praise God for those moments of light and those moments of darkness, for those moments of ease and peace and those moments of difficulty and

---

*Isaiah 45:5, Babylonian Talmud, Brachot 11b
**With gratitude to Rabbi Daniel Siegel for sharing this teaching with me.

discord, perhaps our own journeys will be smoother. It's easy to praise the light, peaceful moments; it's much more difficult to praise the dark, broken times. I remind myself of this challenge daily: How can I hold the joy and effervescence alongside the pain and darkness in our relationships and in our families?

May the Source of All bless us on our journeys to learn to stand in this place of blessing all—the *ohr* and the *choshech*, the *shalom* and the *rah*. As I'm still living through the teenage years, I continue to hold on to this learning—to those days that I am shut out of my daughter's life, as well as those magical days when we lie on her bed together casually chatting about those mundane life topics that, these days, don't ever seem mundane.

Ways to Encourage Respect

1) Speak less. Listen more.
2) Engage in difficult conversations,
respecting each other's perspectives.
3) Watch movies together that present a variety of viewpoints
and discuss together after.
4) If it is in accordance with your family's values, encourage
children to address adults with a surname: Aunt, Uncle, Mr.,
Mrs., Dr., Rabbi, etc.
5) Read a book out loud together that promotes dialogue. Allow
each person to share their viewpoints. Listen to one another
respectfully, asking clarifying questions when appropriate.
6) Hug each other often.

Respect: Questions to Consider

1) Why is respect important?
2) How can we as a family show our respect for one another?
3) Share a time when you felt disrespected. Share a time when
you felt respected.
4) How do we allow our children to grow into who they are meant
to be and still require respect as a family value to be upheld?

Love

(Sh'mah)

א

Sh'mah Yisrael Adonai Eloheinu Adonai Echad

Hear O Israel, Adonai is our God, Adonai is One.

As the mom of three teenagers, I have heard the phrase, "Can you *just* listen!" more than I care to recall. I used to think that I was a decent listener; but these days, it seems as if I can do no right in the listening department. On good days, I'm able to ask, "Do you want me to respond or just listen?" and on not-so-good days, I hear that same refrain, "Can you *just* listen!"

Why is it that I often feel more compelled to talk instead of listen? Maybe because I feel that I have so much that I want to share and impart to my kids before they leave the nest? Maybe I don't want them to make the same "bad" decisions that I made? Or maybe, could it really be to boost my ego? Sometimes I wonder. Over the years, I've come to realize that it is likely a combination of the three, mixed in with some others that have yet to be identified.

When I actually do stop talking and listen, really listen, without an agenda and without anticipating my next remark, something inside me shifts. I notice a spaciousness, a kinder, gentler version of myself. I start to notice the freckles on my daughter's cheeks and the smile on her face. I pay attention to the expressions on my son's face and to the pauses in between his words. With those "noticings," I find that I have more empathy for my teenagers and what they are currently experiencing. Over the years, I've learned that much of love is about listening. Listening to the other, listening to myself, listening to the silence, and listening to that still small voice.*

---

*That still small voice that refers to the Divinity within us. The phrase is from I Kings

I've heard the teaching that "God gave us two ears and one mouth, indicating that we should listen twice as much as we speak." Unfortunately, I would bet that the majority of us do just the opposite, speaking twice as much as we listen. It is interesting to note that the first letter in the Shema prayer is the letter shin, ש which seems to be imparting this wisdom, providing us with a visual of our two ears hiding among the three lines, and inviting us to consider how we use them for listening deeply.

ש

Perhaps there is also another hidden message in this shin. Maybe those lines are space holders, inviting us to remain present and hold steady as the rocky child-rearing years unfold.

Shin... Shhhhh... Shema: Hear/Listen.

Look at the spaces between the lines. Listen for the pauses between the words. Hear the silence between the lines. Be present with the presence of the lines. Even before we get to the rest of this prayer, the quintessential Jewish prayer, that mantra of faith, of Oneness, that has been proclaimed throughout millennia, we are reminded to stop and listen.

Shhhh... Shema... When we begin from a place of deep listening in ourselves and in our relationships, we naturally move toward a place of unity and greater understanding.

I've been working on this with my teenagers, and it is not an easy task. Sometimes they feel like talking, but most of the time they don't. As they arrive home from school, I greet them with questions about their day and usually receive one-word answers; a few sentences if I'm lucky.

Despite my frustration, I remind myself: Be present, just listen to whatever it is they are willing to share. As they disappear into their rooms, log on to their computers, and text their friends, I wonder if they will ever emerge from their caves?

Despite my disappointment, I remind myself again and again to be

---

19:11-12 : "Come out," He called, "and stand on the mountain before God." And, lo, God passed by. There was a great and mighty wind, splitting mountains and shattering rocks by the power of God; but God was not in the wind. After the wind—an earthquake; but God was not in the earthquake; after the earthquake—fire; but God was not in the fire. And after the fire—a soft murmuring sound/a still small voice.

present, and to listen to whatever it is they are willing to share. Most days seem to unfold with a lack of meaningful conversation; and then there are days when I'm preparing dinner in the kitchen and someone wanders in and begins talking. It takes all of my energy *not* to respond. "Stay present and just listen," I tell myself. Making eye contact and nodding my head, I do my best to let them know that they have my attention.

Shin... Shhhh... Shema: Hear/Listen.

I don't always get it right, but I am grateful for what I've learned from that one little letter.

The next time I hear, "Can you just listen!" I will heed my own advice to slow down, listen with both ears, speak half as much as I'd like, and open up my heart to be fully present.

ב

V-ahahvtah et Adonai elohechah, b-chol l'vahv'chah
u'v'chol nahfsh'chah, u'v'chol m'odechah.

**Love Adonai your God with all your heart,
and with all your soul, and with all your might.**

I remember my first week of being a mom with such trepidation and anxiety. As an accomplished professional, I could support myself, cook, clean, and multi-task. I felt pretty sound and grounded in my ability to handle new situations and unforeseen circumstances... and then with the arrival of my first child, my world was rocked. I felt completely deflated and inept. What if I didn't hold him the right way, what if I twisted or moved him too fast, too hard... could I break him? Completely overwhelmed, I literally didn't know which end was up. Thank God, I had been with another dear friend, a year prior, when she was trying to figure out things with her three-day-old daughter. I remember her saying, through her tears, "I am a lawyer, a really competent lawyer, and I can't figure out how to feed my daughter! I think I want to send her back." Now, a year later, I was grateful for having shared that encounter.

After coming home from the hospital, my mother presented me with a photo album that said, "Happiness is being a mother." I thanked her and then burst into tears, thinking to myself, "maybe for other moms but definitely not for me!" She gently hugged me and told me that it would get easier and that one day I would appreciate being a mother.

And like most things, she was right. A few weeks later, with much work—breastfeeding practice, bathing routines, diaper changes, more sleep, an incredibly supportive husband, and a wonderful community of family and friends, I rocked my little Yossi-pie on my shoulder. Even so many years later, I remember the moment, frozen in time: The sun was streaming in through the window. There was a silence immersed in love so deep, so profound, that I knew the love I was experiencing was coming from my soul, connecting to his, and coming from his soul, connecting to mine. At that moment, I had come to understand what it means to love God with all of your soul.

Fast forward two-and-a-half years: I remember being at an open gym, watching my son as he peeked inside one of the windows of a small plastic play house. Suddenly, another child punched him square in the face—for no reason (unless you count opening the window and looking in as a reason), as I looked on in disbelief. At that moment, a feeling I had never in my life experienced began pulsating throughout my entire body. I felt like a mama bear on the war path, about to rage, "Who dares hurt my baby cub?" It was an unbelievably scary moment, and I felt it strongly—love. A love so deep that I would do whatever I had to in order to protect my young. I quickly whisked my son away and gave him hugs and kisses to make it better. At that moment, I had come to understand what it means to love with all of your might.

Now my son is nineteen; he has grown and experienced much more than I could have imagined when I rocked him in that chair and coddled him in that open gym. He has cultivated his own beliefs, values, and philosophies, which are not always in sync with mine. There have been many times over the years when I have lost my temper and didn't think I had another ounce of patience left inside me. I have had to bite my tongue and let him figure things out on his own, and I have spent many a moment in silent prayer asking for help and guidance on what to do with my obstreperous child. Every time I got the same answer: "Open you heart just a little bit wider and love him even more." Not exactly what you want to hear when you really just want to scream. But I accepted this wise inner guidance and did just that. Not always, and not completely successfully, but enough for him to know that I love him unconditionally, with all of my heart.

It has taken me just over a decade to integrate what was written in the *V'ahavta* about how we are to love with all of our heart, all of our soul, and all of our might. Not only are we to love God this way, but I believe this same way of loving applies to our children. Despite the challenges that each of us faces with our children, we ultimately have to open our hearts and souls and love them passionately. For when we have experienced this kind of overwhelming, effusive love that connects body, mind, and spirit with our child, we know that it is possible to love God in the same way. As parents, we strive to love our children totally and completely; and as human beings, we strive to love God with the same totality. The love we share with others will flow back into us, enriching us, helping us become more loving parents and more compassionate people. The more we love, the more love comes our way.

ג

V'sheenahntahm l'vahnechah,
v'deebahrtah bahm, b'shivt'chah b'vaytechah,
u'v'lecht'chah vahderech
u'v'shochb'chah u'v'koomechah.

Impress them upon your children.
Recite them when you stay at home
and when you are away,
when you lie down and when you get up.

Valentine's Day 2017 was just around the corner and my daughter was telling me about a video post she had seen of a 10-year-old girl receiving gifts and chocolates from her boyfriend. I wasn't sure why she was sharing, since she is quite selective about what she shares these days. I remained silent, hoping she would continue talking, and she did, "Can you believe it? She has a boyfriend and she's ten. Well, I know *I* won't be getting anything for Valentine's Day this year."

My heart twinged a bit, feeling her sadness and yet simultaneously grateful that, as a 14-year-old, she did not have a boyfriend.

On February 13, my husband came home from work and surprised both my daughter and me with Godiva chocolates. A rare treat indeed! I was incredibly touched by his thoughtfulness. For the first time, he had bought something for her. I never mentioned the video she had shown me, but it was as if his intuition prompted him to buy her chocolates this year. Knocking on her door, only to receive a "What do you want?!" he kindly responded, "I have something for you, let me know when you can open the door." A few minutes later, she opened her door. In he walked with a golden box in hand. "Thank you so much!" she exclaimed! I knew that she was incredibly touched by his kindness. The next day was February 14. I entered her room to wish her a Happy Valentine's Day with a card and some more chocolates from me. She thanked me, smiled, and said, "Well, I may not have a boyfriend, but I'll always have Dad." Smiling, I responded, "Yes, you will."

As the day progressed, I reflected back upon that moment with deep gratitude on many levels. Grateful that she experienced the thoughtfulness and love of her sweet Dad. Grateful that she was shown how to act toward someone you love. Grateful for knowing the joy of unexpected gifts. The gift of Godiva is one that is extra sweet because of her affinity for this chocolate as a young girl.

My daughter's love for chocolate comes to her honestly, as I am a recovering chocoholic. Not often, but every once in a while, I would splurge and buy myself a couple of Godiva truffles. One day, the golden Godiva box was sitting on my kitchen counter when my then five-year-old, who was learning to read, asked, "Mom, what is that box that says G...G... God..Godv...Godville." Trying my best not to laugh at her and wanting to be sure that I heard her correctly, I asked her to repeat what she said. "Mom, what is in that box that says Godville?" From that day forward, we have called Godiva chocolates *Godville* chocolates. According to my daughter and me, they are **truly** divine!

On the one hand, that funny interpretation is just that—funny; but on the other hand, when I looked deeper, I was happy to see that my daughter could see "God" in a box of chocolates. Having had so many God conversations in our home, this word didn't seem abnormal to her. Growing up, she did have a lot of "God" talk—when we were at home, when we were out in nature, when she got up in the morning, and when she went to bed. God talk was so common that it just seemed "normal" to find God on a box of chocolates.

V-sheenahntahm l-vahnechah, v-deebahrtah bahm,
b-shivt'chah b'vaytechah, oo-v'lecht'chah vahderech
oo-v-shochb'chah oo-v-koomechah

Impress them upon your children. Recite them when you stay at home and when you are away, when you lie down and when you get up.

We read in this prayer that not only are we to love YHVH with all of our heart, mind, and soul, but also, we are to teach our children to do the same, through our speech and our action, at home and away, morning and night. But how do we teach them to love? I'd offer, by simply loving them. We show our children what it means to love YHVH with all of our heart, all of our mind, and all of our soul by loving *them* with all of our **heart**, all of our **mind**, and all of our **soul**.

Some may ask, how does one love on all of those levels—heart, mind, and soul? Jokingly, I respond: Eat some chocolate—it reaches all of those places. A more serious response might include that loving someone with your heart means using your emotional capacity to make them happy. Loving someone with your mind means using your intellect and knowledge to make them happy. Loving someone with your soul means using your "sixth sense" or intuition to make them happy. When we are able to combine all of these levels into an action, into a word, into a gesture, then we are showing our children how we love them fully, which then becomes a reflection of how we are able to love God.

Those Godiva chocolates were a true expression of my husband's deep love for our daughter. He used his heart, his mind, and his soul in his choice of what to purchase, when, and why. To some, it may seem like he just bought her a box of chocolates, but I believe that to her that box represented something deeper, perhaps even something she was not able to see yet. Wrapped up in that box of Godville chocolates were God-infused conversations, memories, sweetness, thoughtfulness, and deep, deep love.

Love: Questions to Consider

1) How would you assess your listening ability? What might you do to improve it?
2) How do you express love for your child?
3) Dr. Gary Chapman writes about five love languages. He teaches that each person receives and experiences love most fully in one of five ways: affirmation, physical touch, gifts, acts of service, or quality time.* What makes you feel most loved? How about your partner? Your child?

Ways to Promote Love

1) Learn the "love language" of each of your family members (see above).
2) Leave love notes for your beloveds in unexpected places (dresser drawers, lunch boxes, purses, wallets, desktops, etc.).
3) Listen deeply...without responding immediately.
4) Make time each day to spend at least a few minutes alone with your child.

---

*Chapman, Gary D. *The 5 Love Languages: The Secret to Love that Lasts*. Illinois: Northfield Publishing, 1992.

Empowerment
(Mee Chamocha)

א

Mee chamochah bah-aylim Adonai?
mee kamochah nedahr bah-kodesh?

Who is like you, Adonai, among all that is worshiped?
Who is like you, majestic in holiness?

Several years back, my kids had an obsession with perler beads, the little plastic beads that when placed on a template and ironed stick together to form various shapes. Over the years, my daughter must have made nearly one hundred items: animals, geometric shapes, Jewish stars, dolphins, ice cream cones, and the list goes on. One year, two of my children asked to sell them at our synagogue's annual Hanukkah Talent Show. They checked with the rabbi, promised to donate a percentage back to the synagogue, and set up a booth. Selling their items for a small fee—ranging from fifty cents to two dollars—over the course of the night, they made close to $40, of which eight was donated. They each got to keep $16, an amount which to an eight- and a ten-year-old translates into a lot of hard-earned money. My kids were thrilled and proud of their accomplishment, as was I.

They learned so much from this empowering experience. I love how they dove right in, figuring out their material costs, sorting the perler beads into price categories, making signage for advertising, keeping track of their sales, and donating a percentage back to the synagogue.

After they were done, my daughter and I walked next door to the pizza place. As we were waiting for her slice, she noticed a March of Dimes stand with some pictures of babies that read, "Every coin makes a difference in the life of a child." It was half-filled with quarters. She immediately reached into her newly earned bag of coins and asked if she could donate some. Here she had just earned $16 and felt moved and empowered to help other kids. She carefully took the quarters out of her plastic bag and excitedly placed them, one by one, into the slots on the stand. She was beaming.

What an incredible offering from her heart. I couldn't have been prouder! Remember back to when you were a kid and had a few hard earned dollars in your pocket? I sure do, and as her mom, I could feel her sense of empowerment in knowing that she had worked hard, earned money, and now used this money to make a difference in the life of another child.

Mee chamochah bah-aylim Adonai?
mee kamochah nedahr bah-kodesh?

Who is like you, Adonai, among all that is worshiped?
Who is like you, majestic in holiness?

This prayer derives from an exact quote in the Torah.* The Israelites had been freed by Pharaoh and had arrived at the shore of the Sea of Reeds, which they were unable to cross. As they waited by the edge, they heard Pharaoh's army approaching in the distance. After releasing the Israelites, Pharaoh had changed his mind. Realizing how difficult life in Egypt would be without his slave workers, he decided to chase after the Israelites in an attempt to bring them back to Egypt. Faced with the waters in front of them and the Egyptians behind them, the Israelites began to panic. How could they possibly escape?

The Midrash tells the tale of Nachshon ben Amminadav, who bravely stepped into the waters, reciting the words *"Mee chahmochah bah-aylim Adonai."* The first letter in the second word, "chah," has a guttural pronunciation (imagine the sound one makes when something is stuck in their throat). The rabbis describe Nachshon walking into the water, the level as high as his throat. When he recites this phrase, the water floods into his mouth, but he does not fear. He continues on, and as he recites the second line, *"Mee kah-mochah nedahr bah-kodesh,"* the waters miraculously part; he then recites the first letter of the second word: "kah" (without

---

*Exodus 15:11

the guttural sound), signifying to us that the water has receded. The similarity of these two letters, "chah" and "kah," is remarkable. Through the Midrash, we come to learn of Nachshon's great faith and his sense of empowerment—taking the first step needed to move the crowd forward.

Seeing my daughter taking the steps to jump right in and donate some *tzedakah* toward this beautiful cause made my heart sing. This process toward her empowerment—creating her own revenue stream and then having the ability to donate immediately—brought me such joy. After she had deposited many coins, she looked up at me and said, "Mom, it says that every coin makes a difference."

Hearing this from her perspective was truly eye-opening. As an adult, donating 25 cents seems like *Mee chamochah* —trying to wade through a sea that is up to our throats—there is no way one quarter can help; and then hearing my daughter's remarks moved me to *Mee kamochah*—an opening of waters parting—every coin makes a difference. Experiencing this with my daughter taught me that through the process of empowerment, we have the power to jump in, act purposefully, and truly make a difference in the lives of others.

בּ

Norah t'heelot, osei feleh.

Awesome in splendor, working wonders.

Sometimes it truly takes a miracle, maybe even some Divine Intervention, to patch up a difficult friendship.

In fourth grade my daughter had a friend who was like a sister to her; unfortunately, their relationship encompassed many of those sibling emotions of love and hate. Each day after school, I would wait to hear the drama from the day: what happened during lunch, who didn't sit next to whom, who "accidentally" poked whom, who was picked to be on whose soccer team, and the list went on. Most days were filled with tears and great frustration.

Listening patiently, I suggested that perhaps she might want to find a different friend.

"No, Mom, I really like her, a lot."

"OK, I hear you, but it seems like you are continually having problems. Maybe you should take a break from one another."

"No, I don't want to. We really like hanging out."

"Hmmm... maybe you should hang out but try not to sit next to one another in class."

"Uh-uh, we like working together."

"Ah-ha. Ok, let me get this straight. Nearly every day, you have a fight with Debbie*, and you still want to sit next to her in class, hang out with her, and get together on the weekends. Am I missing something?"

"Nope. Never mind, forget it, you don't understand!"

I was at a loss for words, unable to comprehend this situation. Clearly, I was not able to help my daughter with this difficult friendship. Feeling bereft, all I could do was prepare myself for the dose of Daily Drama.

Several months passed, and there would be "good" months and "bad" months. In the "good" months, the girls didn't fight, but in the "bad" months, well, let's just say it was BAD! Debbie's mother and I had spoken on occasion, but one day we happened to bump into each other, coincidentally... or not. We have very different schedules and rarely see one another. Since our daughters had been friends for several years, we had shared friendly conversations and had enough of a relationship to mention to one another the difficulties that our daughters were experiencing with each other. Once we began sharing our perspectives, it became apparent that the girls truly loved each other and wanted to be friends but lacked the social savvy or communication skills to make it happen.

And so the two of us concocted a plan. What if we could get our daughters to sit down and talk to one another, to share their feelings and frustrations openly, with the moms guiding the conversation? Could we actually pull this off? We each spoke to our respective daughters, suggesting a "pow-wow" where the four of us would meet and create a safe space for each to share what was on her mind.

By the grace of God, awesome in splendor, working wonders—the girls actually agreed! *Norah t'heelot, osei feleh.* I am not sure what actually

---

*Name changed to protect identity.

prompted them to say yes—our cavalier attitudes or their realization that they were both suffering from this dysfunctional, unhealthy friendship. But in our minds, the fact that they said "yes!" was truly a miracle, not to mention the fact that our mom-happenstance-meeting was highly unlikely.

It did feel a bit like the Universe was in cahoots and wanted these girls to work out their friendship kinks. And yet, with all of these strange coincidences, what Debbie's mom and I wanted most of all was to provide our daughters with a venue to express themselves, to empower them to speak their individual truths—not knowing if they would manage to resolve their problems or not. Planning this meeting was an act of faith because we, too, were entering unchartered and unknown territory. We were like the Israelites standing at the shore of the Sea of Reeds, measuring the cost-benefit analysis ratio. Should we jump in together, not knowing the outcome, or should we wait passively for something else to happen?

Both of us felt that the potential outcome was worth the risk, and so we arranged a meeting at Debbie's house. We figured, at the very least, if it was a total disaster, we would be providing our daughters with an important life skill in conflict management and communication skills.

As my daughter and I were welcomed into Debbie's house, we began with some small talk until Debbie's mom invited us into the dining room, where the girls sat next to each other and the moms sat across from them. We laid out the ground rules:
- one person talks at a time
- everyone listens carefully
- no interrupting
- no making fun of someone
- be honest and kind

The girls handled the conversation beautifully, each empowered to speak her truth and her feelings. They explained to one another how it felt when the other one behaved in a hurtful manner. They were introspective and used kind words. What an empowering moment for our daughters! They spoke their true feelings, they had those feeling validated, and then they came up with a plan so they could avoid the pitfalls they had each caused along the way. I am grateful to Debbie's mom for partnering with me to craft this "empowerment session" for our daughters. I'm even happier to share that eight years later the girls are still dear friends. Having worked through their challenges, their miraculous friendship is stronger than ever.

ג

Shirah chahdahshah shib'chu ge'uleem

The redeemed sang a new song for You.

I pulled into the gas station only to find one of its entrances blocked by a tanker trailer. Making my way around the parking lot, I found another entry point and pulled up next to the pump. As I filled my car up with gas, I watched the workman detaching and re-attaching the hoses on his truck. Lining them up, readying all that needed to be properly aligned in order to fill up the underground lines with gas.

My initial thought was, "Cool, a tanker trailer; I actually know what kind of truck that is." Until 16 years ago, it would have just been a truck. Never one to have learned the names of various trucks, a truck was a truck. That is, until my oldest came along with his truck obsession. He wasn't satisfied with just *truck*; rather, he wanted to know the precise name for each truck. Oh my, I was ill-prepared for this part of parenting!

Thank goodness for grandparents who, upon learning about Yossi's truck fascination, sent him a book detailing trucks: tanker trailer, eighteen wheeler, front-loader, backhoe, flatbed, just to name a few. Each day we read and re-read his Tonka Truck Book and I began to speak a new language, literally and figuratively. As we drove down the road, I was able to speak my son's "truck language," identifying surrounding vehicles and connecting with him in a way that previously had not been possible.

As I sat in my car, I reflected back to 16 years ago, when this tanker trailer filling up at the gas pumps would have been an "activity" for us. I would have pulled off to the side, parked while we watched the entire process, and answered myriad questions that were sure to follow. Instead, I would fill up my car up and drive off to my errands.

This is what flooded my mind that morning as I waited for my tank to fill up.

And then I lost it; the tears began rolling down my face. Seemingly out of nowhere, they continued until I was sobbing. Quickly getting into my car, I cried inside until I heard the gas pump click, put on sunglasses, and finished up outside before returning to my car in tears.

What had just happened? It didn't take too long for me to figure out that I had just been triggered—looking at a tanker trailer had whisked me back into the past. I lost it. I was transported back in time. Wondering where the years had gone. My son, entering his senior year, is applying to colleges. He's about to take a leap, a really, really big leap! I have a feeling that it's going to be one of those years filled with memories—you know, the selective memories of how wonderful and idyllic life was raising him. For sure, there have been challenging times, but somehow at this moment they faded into the background and what came to the foreground was that it is almost time for him to fly the coop.

I am happy for him. Really, I am. I'm excited for him to go out and fly, to be independent, to discover his gifts, to experience successes and failures. But sometimes my genuine excitement is overshadowed by my knowing that our relationship will change and that this is the beginning of the end of our "mother-teenage son living under one roof" relationship. I remember when he was born. Wasn't it just a few years ago?

I wonder if God felt similarly when the Israelites were re-birthed from slaves to free people. How would their relationship change now that they were no longer enslaved? Would they still call out to God in the same way or would their ways of communicating shift? The Slonimer Rebbe, a 20th century Hasidic rabbi,* teaches that the slavery experienced by the Israelites did indeed change the way in which God and the Israelites communicated. According to him, the Israelites were not able to speak while they were enslaved because slavery had encompassed their entire being, including their speech. They had no ability for words; they were not able to call out for redemption. They were not even able to pray. All they could do was sigh and cry.**

But God heard their moaning and answered them. With the arrival of Moses on the scene and the unfolding of the Ten Plagues, the Israelites

---

*His given name was Sholom Noah Berezovsky, b. 1911-d. 2000.
** Exodus 2:23.

were freed. Now, as they stood at the shore of the Sea of Reeds, waiting to cross over, the water was too deep, and they were unable to pass. This time, they called out—in words—*Mee chahmochah*—Who is like You? The words continuing to pour out of their mouths, *Sheerah chahdahshah shib'chu ge'uleem:* the redeemed sing a new song.

In the midst of their singing, I can't help but wonder what was going through their minds. Were they musing about life on the other side of the sea? Wondering if life would be better than before? In Egypt, they knew what to expect. Now, as free people, the unknown must have been paralyzing. Did they even want to cross? Of course, you say, who wouldn't want to be free? But as we know, freedom, too, comes at a price. Sometimes there are too many choices and not enough structure. The lack of boundaries and routine can be daunting.

History was made. Miraculously, the sea parted and the redeemed sang a new song to God. A song filled with joy and affirmation, gratitude, excitement, and, I'd like to contend, a bit of trepidation. Yes, they had been redeemed, but they were off to begin a new, unknown segment of their journey.

As I sat in that parking lot, I thought a lot about the next part of my son's journey. Proverbially, he is standing at the Sea of Reeds. I'm sure he has felt a bit like a "slave" to our rules, and I know he can't wait to get out of our house so he can make his own choices.

Reflecting back, I hope that we have empowered him to communicate effectively, to learn new vocabulary when needed, and to share his thoughts and feelings. I hope that somewhere stored in the deep recesses of his memory he remembers a time when his mom had to learn a new language, with new terminology, in order to speak to her son's growing curiosity.

As my son crosses over to the unknown, I imagine that we both feel joy and affirmation, gratitude, excitement, and a bit of trepidation. Neither one of us knows what the future holds, and yet we have faith that everything will be okay even in the midst of the unknown. Anxiously, I await and look forward to experiencing the new song my "redeemed" son sings as he ventures out into the world.

Ways to Empower

1) Encourage your child to try something new.
2) Take a family trip to an unfamiliar place.
3) Acknowledge fear. Embolden courage.
4) Find a family hobby that requires everyone to stretch a bit. For example, if you've never tried camping—try it! If you don't feel comfortable cooking or baking—try it!
5) Visit a nursing home or old age home and have your child bring along some homemade cards or art and crafts trinkets to distribute.

Empowerment: Questions to Consider

1) How does it feel to be empowered?
2) Discuss a time when you felt disempowered. Now discuss a time when you felt empowered. What was the difference between the two?
3) Why is empowerment important and what role can it play in your life?
4) Ask your child their opinion about age-appropriate important topics, such as politics, God, sex, friendship, the environment, etc., and have discussions about them. Empower them to speak out and allow them to be heard.

Family

(Amidah)

א

Baruch ahtah Adonai eloheinu
vay-lohay eemoteinu v-ahvoteinu
Elohei Ahvrah'hahm Elohei Sahrah
Elohei Yitschahk Elohei Rivkah
Elohei Yah'ahkov Elohei Leah vay-lohay Rahchel

We praise you, Adonai our God and God of all generations:
God of Abraham, God of Sarah,
God of Isaac, God of Rebecca,
God of Jacob, God of Leah, and God of Rachel

Every year on Rosh Hashanah, I make my Gigi's (Grandma's) apple cake. When she passed away in 2001, I was able to take a few of her cookbooks and kitchen utensils. The first time I baked her cake, I used her tube pan. The smell wafting out from my oven took me back to my childhood. I immediately called my mom and screamed into the phone, "My house smells like Gigi's!"

Since then, Gigi's Apple Cake has made a name for itself, and my kids look forward to eating it each year at Rosh Hashanah. Yes, they are excited for apples and honey and for blowing the shofar, but most importantly for Gigi's Apple Cake. The cake is such a hit that one year my daughter finally inquired, "Why we do we have to wait for Rosh Hashanah to arrive? Why can't we eat it all year round?" I offered to make Gigi's Vegetable Soup year round—but that didn't have the same appeal.

When I prepare her recipes, I talk about my grandmother and share her wisdom and adages with my children. My daughter, who is named for my grandmother, shares a special posthumous relationship with her and enjoys hearing "Gigi stories." Every time my daughter asks me if I can cook without onions, I share that I, too, felt the same way as a child and asked my Gigi why she had to cook with onions. "Couldn't you just leave them out?" to which she responded, "Honey, the key to any good recipe is the onions. You need to start with browning an onion; it gives it a good flavor and then you don't even taste it." Stories like that connect generations.

Hearing stories is one thing, but seeing pictures and hearing people's voices is quite another. For the first few years when our children were young, they didn't join my husband and me when we watched our wedding video on our anniversary; however, as the years have passed, they've taken to joining us. Unfortunately, with the passing of time comes the passing of loved ones. More and more of our older relatives are no longer alive, and these few moments on screen are all that we have left as visual memories. Listening to the voices of my grandparents and seeing them on our television is bittersweet. I miss them so much, and as I sit there with tears streaming down my face, my children can sense the importance of my relationships with them. We often share funny stories about their great-grandparents in the hope that they, too, will come to understand their roots and the values that have been transmitted through me to them.

When my oldest son became a bar mitzvah, he received a most prized gift. One of my husband's relatives from Croatia gave him a watch with the initials JP. This watch belonged to my son's great-great-grandfather, with whom he shared the name. Our relative told us that when he inherited this watch he was unsure of what to do with it; nonetheless, he figured he would hold onto it until the right opportunity presented itself.

When he received an invitation to our son's bar mitzvah, he knew that our son, JP, was the rightful heir to the JP watch. Seeing the look of awe on my usually non-emotive son was extremely touching. In that moment, I sensed that he understood the depth and importance of his roots. We all stand on the shoulders of those who came before us; we are here because of the love, perseverance, and dedication of our ancestors. Later, we spoke about the watch and how cool it is that it has been in our family for many decades; even more amazing is how during difficult times, such as World War I and World War II, no one in the family sold the watch, which could have been used for food or bribes. I'm certain that this beautiful family heirloom and its story will remain in my son's heart forever.

Building upon the generations that came before us, tapping into their strengths and merits, is a central theme in the Amidah prayer. Within the first few words, we connect ourselves to our ancestors: Abraham and Sarah; Isaac and Rebecca; and Jacob, Rachel, and Leah. After offering our praise to God, but before any additional praises, requests, or thanks, we link ourselves first and foremost to our ancestors. The words in this prayer immediately connect us to our past, to those who came before.

In helping our children grow into successful adults, I believe it is important to link them to their past, to help them have a deep understanding of their family's history, stories, and values. So often, my kids question me, "Why do we have to do this? Why do you make us do that?" And while I might prefer to answer, "because I said so," I know that answer is not satisfactory for them. If I share, "Because it was important to my parents, and my grandparents," oftentimes arguments or conflicts dissipate.

We live in a fast-moving, instant gratification, technologically advanced culture that values speed and ease. Baking my Gigi's Apple Cake is the antithesis. It requires more than two hours of time to prepare and bake. It requires peeling lots of apples, mixing dry ingredients, mixing wet ingredients, using lots of bowls, layering apples and batter, and baking for two hours. It would be much faster to run to the supermarket and buy an apple cake. But for sure, it wouldn't be as tasty; more importantly, it wouldn't mean as much to me or to my kids. There is something magical about slowing down and connecting to our loved ones who are no longer among us.

When my son takes out his JP watch, he won't be using it to tell time, as it no longer works. It is missing parts that most likely can't be replaced. But as he holds the gold watch in his hand and watches it glisten in the light, he will think back about his connection to his great-great-grandfather.

Linking our children to their past provides them with roots, roots that help ground them in the uncertainty of life. Knowing that there were those who came before, who had similar challenges, dreams, and thoughts, provides a sense of comfort and security. Things may be very different for our children than they were for children decades ago, but family and its importance is something that will never grow old.

ב

Baruch ahtah Adonai eloheinu
vay-lohay eemoteinu v-ahvoteinu
Elohei Ahvrah'hahm Elohei Sahrah
Elohei Yitschahk Elohei Rivkah
Elohei Yah'ahkov Elohei Leah vay-lohay Rahchel

We praise you, Adonai our God and God of all generations:
God of Abraham, God of Sarah,
God of Isaac, God of Rebecca,
God of Jacob, God of Leah, and God of Rachel

Each year as we give our Hanukkah presents, I make sure to calculate the dollar amount that I spend on each of my children. I know it sounds crazy, but it is actually something that I learned from my mom. If she spends $25 on one of her children, she will ensure that she spends $25 on the other two. If she can't find a gift she likes for the $25, she will find a gift for $20 and put the extra five dollars in the card. She is really serious about being fair with all of her children and grandchildren and, for better or worse, it has rubbed off on me. So, I am sure to spend an equal sum total, even if the individual gifts range in price. I am notorious for saying to my kids, "Everything works out in the end," meaning that I try my best to keep a running mental tab, and while you may want shoes because your brother is getting them now, yours still fit you and you'll get new shoes when you need them. If one son gets to lick the batter this time around, next time someone else will get the honors. I know my decisions and actions can drive my kids crazy, but I try to be as equitable as I can.

I try to abide by the same principles when disciplining my kids: equal consequences for equal infringements. Of course, I always hear, "That's not fair, you always punish me more than you punish her!" "That's not fair, last time when I said a curse word, I was grounded for a month; why is he only grounded for a week?" The grievances go on and on... In reality, as much as I try to police with equity, I am human and no doubt have occasionally erred. Frankly, if truth be told, I just don't remember from one punishment to the next. I know my kids well enough to know who instigates more often, who tattles most frequently, who wants attention, and who, based on past history, is most likely to be guilty of the crime. And, as much as I might not want to admit it, I am sure that somewhere in the mix is a bit of my subjectivity.

We read in the opening lines of the Amidah that God, too, has unique relationships with each of His children. The first line of this prayer can be divided into three parts:

Baruch ahtah Adonai Eloheinu
vay-lohay eemoteinu v-ahvoteinu,
Elohei Ahvrah'hahm Elohei Sahrah,
Elohei Yitschahk Elohei Rivkah,
Elohei Yah'ahkov Elohei Leah vay-lohay Rahchel

We praise you, Adonai our God and God of all generations:
God of Abraham, God of Sarah,
God of Isaac, God of Rebecca
God of Jacob, God of Leah, and God of Rachel

It is interesting to note that the prayer doesn't say *Elohei Ahvrah'hahm, Yitschahk, and Yah'ahkov*—God of Abraham, Isaac, and Jacob, or *Elohei Sahrah, Rivkah, Leah, and Rahchel*, God of Sarah, Rebecca, Leah, and Rachel. Rather, the words acknowledge that God had a unique, individual relationship with each patriarch and each matriarch: *Elohei Ahvrah'hahm, Elohei Yitschahk, V'ay-lohay Yah'ahkov*, God of Abraham, God of Isaac, and God of Jacob; *Elohei Sarah, Elohei Rivkah, Elohei Leah, Vei-lohei Rahchel*, God of Sarah, God of Rebecca, God of Leah, and God of Rachel.

Each patriarch had different experiences with God and viewed God uniquely. Just as in our families, each of our children experiences us and sees us differently. Even though we think we act the same toward each child, the way each child perceives us is different. I often wonder how my children are so different if I raised them all similarly? And I know from talking to my friends that they, too, ponder this same question.

However, if I have to be honest, I know there are times that although I think I am treating each child the same, I'm not. I can't because they all have varying temperaments and dispositions. I learned early on that while one way of disciplining may work with one of my children, it most certainly will not work with all of them. Although I would like to be described as Mother of Yossi, Eitan, and Bat-Ella, it would be more accurate and honest to be described as Mother of Yossi, Mother of Eitan, and Mother of Bat-Ella. Reflecting on my own parenting, I have to acknowledge that while I try really hard to be an across-the-board mother, in reality, I am not. Reading the words of the Amidah reminds me that just as I can learn about God by examining God's unique, individual relationship with each of the patriarchs—Abraham, Isaac, and Jacob—and with each of the matriarchs—Sarah, Rebecca, Leah, and Rachel—I can also learn about myself by examining my relationship with each of my children.

The Kabbalists (Jewish mystics) associate a specific character trait with each patriarch: Abraham with *chesed*, or loving-kindness; Isaac with *gevurah*, or might/restraint; and Jacob with *tiferet*, or beauty/balance.

We learn about their individual relationships with God from the stories in the Torah and the Midrash. We read about Abraham's generosity when he welcomed strangers into his tent, providing them with food and water. Due to this kindness, his wife Sarah, who had been struggling with infertility, was blessed to become pregnant.* We also read about Abraham's generosity of spirit when he argued with God to save the lives of strangers whose lives were slated for destruction in the towns of Sodom and Gomorrah.**

Isaac, known for his might and restraint, is defined by his binding, known in Hebrew as the *Akeda*. Isaac followed his father, Abraham, up to the mountains with wood and kindling, wondering where the as-yet unfound ram was to be sacrificed. It was Isaac's discipline and his ability to continue walking the path with his father, not knowing to where he was being led, that characterizes Isaac's inner fortitude. Through his withholding, not lashing out and screaming, "Where are you taking me?" Isaac's *gevurah*, might or strength, becomes paramount.

---

* Genesis 18:10.
** Genesis 18:17-33.

Jacob comes to bring balance between loving-kindness and might through their integration and through creation of *tiferet*, or beauty. What he learned from his father, Isaac (represented as *gevurah*), and grandfather, Abraham (represented as *chesed*), was that too much of one trait does not work. Overflowing love without boundaries, or intense strictness without love, cannot sustain a relationship. There must be balance—love with boundaries and strictness with love.

As a parent, this message of Jacob's *tiferet*, balance, is both timely and helpful. I remember my time spent as a classroom teacher. I saw children whose parents were incredibly loving and doting—so much so, that they were incapable of setting limits. I also saw the other extreme: parents who were so strict that the rules always superseded love, understanding, and compassion. Neither of these scenarios resulted in healthy, well-adjusted children. Like everything in life, balance is necessary. The challenge is to love fully with limits and be strict with compassion.

By reflecting on our ancestors who represent the traits of *chesed, gevurah,* and *tiferet*, we can learn about ourselves as parents and work toward finding the middle ground of balance—of *tiferet*—of compassion, beauty and splendor. It is through these traits and stories that we see God's unique relationships with our patriarchs. The *Kabbalah* teaches that while these traits are representative of our ancestors, they are also traits that are reflective of God, and of ourselves.

By looking at our own parenting and reflecting on how *chesed, gevurah,* and *tiferet* appear in our parenting styles, we can better guide our children to find those qualities in themselves. By modeling *chesed*—loving-kindness—random acts of kindness, without expecting anything in return, we teach our children its true meaning. By establishing boundaries and holding fast to rules, our children will be able to establish and recognize safe boundaries and environments. They will come to understand the importance of *gevurah*, might and restraint. By teaching the importance of balance—not always saying yes and not always saying no—by allowing our children to choose a couple of favorite extracurricular activities and by encouraging them to eat a well-balanced diet, we will help them find the middle ground in making decisions and acting in balance. By finding the right space and place for these traits and making sure to aim for the center, in terms of when to use them, we will move our children toward *tiferet*, harmony and balance.

God of Abraham, God of Isaac, and God of Jacob, God of Sarah, God of Rebecca, God of Leah, and God of Rachel, thank you for teaching us the importance of *chesed*, *gevurah*, and *tiferet* and for allowing us the insight to guide our children successfully on their path to adulthood as we reflect on our own strengths, weaknesses, and relationships.

Ways to Develop Importance of Family

1) Find time during the week to spend time as a family. If that can't work, try to find several times a month.
2) Look at old photo albums or old family videos together.
3) Tell family stories. Kids especially love to hear stories about their parents as youngsters.
4) Create a memory book or scrapbook for your family, both nuclear and extended.
5) If your children were named after a relative, teach them for whom they were named and what qualities you hope they will emulate.
6) Strive to eat dinner together on a regular basis. If scheduling is too crazy, try to eat Shabbat dinner together.
7) If you have them, frame old family photos to display in your house.

Family: Questions to Consider

1) How do you share your family's history with your children?
2) What family traits are you most proud of? How can you integrate them into your family?
3) What is your overall approach to parenting in terms of *chesed, gevurah, tiferet*? Are there times when you see one being more applicable than another?
4) How can you strive for *tiferet*, balance? What scaffolding do you need to put in place in order for you to be balanced as a person and as a parent? How can you carve out individual time, couple time, family time?

ג

Melech ozeir umoshi'a umahgein
Baruch ahtah Adonai
mahgein Ahvrahahm ufokeid Sarah.

Sovereign, who helps, and saves and shields.
You are praised, Adonai,
shield of Abraham and rememberer of Sarah

Several years ago, when my oldest was about seven, our aunt and uncle were visiting from Israel. Although we call them aunt and uncle, they are really more like grandparents toward my kids. They are doting and loving, and spoil them like their own biological grandkids. One afternoon, I was preparing lunch for my children and my son started to complain about what I had chosen to make.

After all these years, I can no longer remember the exact reason (perhaps it was the choice of whole wheat bread, or maybe I added too much peanut butter to the PB&J), but whatever the reason, I turned to my uncle and blurted out, "Just for one day, I wish he didn't have food to eat.

Just for one day, for him to know what it is like to be so hungry that he wouldn't complain about the food!" With patience, and an open heart, my Uncle Yossi replied, "Please, Amy, don't ever wish that for your child. I was just that child. I had to scrounge through garbage cans to find food to eat during the War. It is a terrible thing; no matter how angry you get at him, please don't ever wish that for your child."

Silence.

Since that experience, I have thought a lot about what he shared with me. His message was about protection, and about making sure that my kids are safe, with their primary needs met.

When my kids were toddlers, each of them went through a phase where they were scared that there were monsters in their rooms. Every night at bedtime, they would procrastinate, ask for a nightlight, whine and cry, and beg us to stay with them until they fell asleep. When we asked why, we were told "because of the monsters."

I was talking to a good friend of mine, asking if she had any ideas, and she suggested something that worked for her kids: Monster Spray. She instructed me to get a clear spray bottle and label it in black ink with the words MONSTER SPRAY, fill it with water, and bring it to my kids at bedtime. I explained to them that I had gone to the store and bought a special spray that would keep away the monsters. At first, they didn't believe me, but I quickly shared with them the guidelines under which it worked. First, only the one who sees the monsters can spray it. And second, you had to hiss at the monsters to get them away while you were spraying. On the first night of usage, my son and I tried it out and it worked! Every subsequent night, he asked for the spray and voilà, the monsters didn't bother him anymore.

It was through this process of empowering him that he connected to his inner strength and became almost like the superheroes he was used to watching on TV. He transformed into one of the Rescue Heroes, chasing away the bad guys and saving the day, or the night, as it were.

Consider the words in the *Amidah*—*Melech ozeir umoshi'a umahgain*— God, you are the One who helps, saves, and protects. It is interesting to look at the layering of these words: One who helps, saves, and protects. First, God can help from afar (*ozeir*), then perhaps a bit closer to save (*umoshi'a*), and finally right next to us with protection (*umahgein*). As parents, I believe that we can behave the same way toward our children. Sometimes we help, sometimes we save, and sometimes we protect. As our children mature, I'd offer that this layering works better as an inverse formula. When our kids are really young, we want to be right next to them, protecting and shielding (*umahgein*) them from any harm. As they get older, we may jump in to save (*umoshi'a*) them at specific times of need. Finally, we hope that ultimately we will be a helping hand (*ozeir*) as they learn to navigate life on their own.*

I'm not quite sure where the monster spray fits into this layering. I'm just glad it worked.

---

*I thank my dear friend Shoshana Gross for sharing this insight.

Peace

(Sim Shalom)

א

Sim Shalom. Grant Peace.

Damn! I thought I was doing the right thing, but in retrospect I think I failed big-time. It is not often that my teenage daughter engages in conversation, and it is even less frequent when that conversation involves her feelings and vulnerabilities. So when she asked me to come to her room to talk, I quickly made myself available. Excited to hear what was on her mind and her heart, I listened carefully, not interrupting, trying to take in what she was sharing.

In a few weeks she would be starting a new school as a freshman, and she was contemplating trying out for the soccer team. She's been playing soccer since she was three, and it is one of her passions, but this school team had a great reputation and she was afraid that she wouldn't make the team. Even if she did make the team, she wondered aloud if she'd be relegated to playing "bench." "Maybe I shouldn't try out at all," she asked.

I wanted to scream, "What are you talking about?! You're an amazing player; you've been playing your entire life. Why would you even consider that?" But I kept silent and let her continue talking. The more she talked, the harder it became to remain quiet, and so I began asking her questions. "Why wouldn't you try out? Are you afraid you won't make the team? Do you think it will be too time-consuming and you won't be able to get your work done? Are you afraid you'll get hurt?" And if all of these assailing questions weren't bad enough, I heard her whisper, "and I don't want to upset Dad."

"What did you say?"

"Nothing."

"I know you said something."

"Then why are you asking what I said, if you already heard me?"

"Because I wanted to be sure. Why do you think Dad would be upset if you didn't try out for the team?"

"Because I'm the youngest, and it will be his last chance to watch any of us play soccer for school."

"I think he'll be okay with whatever you decide."

"I don't. I think he would be really upset if I didn't play. I mean, I'm the last one who will have the chance to play and I know how much he loves soccer and he always tells us how much he loves watching us play and I don't want to disappoint him. I don't want to let him down."

Some tears began to trickle down her cheek. My heart began to ache more and more with each passing tear. I wanted her to share her feelings with her dad. While I was able to listen to her, I wanted to bring peace and resolution to this dilemma and figured the best way to do this was for the two of them to talk. I made the suggestion to her and got a resounding "NO!"

More tears. More tears. More tears.

Once more, I asked her to go talk to her dad and she still didn't want to. I went to bring my husband into her room, hoping to get them to talk. (Very bad move on my part!) Well, as you might imagine, the rest of the conversation didn't go so well. Even though my husband was able to coerce my daughter into sharing her feelings, and even though he did a wonderful job of calming her fears and beautifully sharing that she should try out for the team only if she wanted to, in hindsight, I shouldn't have opened my mouth. I thought I was doing the right thing, desperately wanting to bring peace to their relationship, but I wound up causing damage to my own relationship with my daughter.

In this prayer, we read the words *sim shalom*, often translated as "grant peace," but literally meaning "place peace." That was my desire, to place peace in my daughter's mind and heart and in the relationship between her and her dad. Perhaps if I had taken the time to reflect more clearly on the word shalom and thought about its root meaning—wholeness, completeness—I would have realized that it is the job of the individual to create a sense of wholeness in oneself. Creating wholeness is an inside job; it can't be done by someone else. By trying to make peace for my daughter, I was not being helpful. In fact, sadly, I think I actually caused harm by taking away her own sense of wholeness. How I wish I had sat quietly and allowed her to come to her own conclusions about creating a sense of wholeness for herself.

We ask God to bring peace to our world, and as we ask God to do this work, I have come to understand that it actually starts with us. Each of us is responsible for bringing peace to our own individual lives. Each of us must work toward wholeness and authenticity, and when we do so, our world will then reflect *shleimut*—wholeness and integration.

Which brings me back to my daughter, and my attempt to do the work for her. I regret my decision that night, and when I checked in with her a few days later to see if my decision to "put peace" upon her was indeed a mistake, she confirmed my suspicions.

Note to self: Next time, just listen, smile, love, hug, listen more, and allow your children to create their own inner peace so that their internal landscape becomes a reflection of the wholeness of the Universe.

ב

Sim Shalom tovah oo–v'rahchah, chein vah-chesed, v–rahchahmeem ahleinu

Grant peace, well-being and blessing, life, grace, love, and mercy for us.

I want it back... all of it... every moment. The times when I was ready to pull my hair out wondering what other "activity" we could possibly do, and it was only noon? The jumping and running and yelling and pushing and punching and biting. The diaper changes and nighttime baths. The middle-of-the-night exhausting feedings. The hugs and kisses and bedtime snuggles. The insult hurling and book throwing and tantrum throwing days. The very, very long days and the very, very short years. I want them back—all of them.

I finally have a quiet house tonight. The kind of quiet that I have dreamt about for years. Quiet for me to do whatever I want, to move slowly, deliberately, and mindfully. As I prepare for Shabbat, I find myself alone, and while I love the quiet, I'm not quite ready for this stage of my life. My daughter is out of town at a soccer tournament, one son is at a friend's house, and my husband and other son are at a gig. All of my men will be home for dinner, and yet, I'm struck by how I got to this place.

As my oldest son walked out the door, with guitar in hand, I was struck by how handsome he has become. It's not that I don't notice that he has a slight beard and a man's physique, it's just that something hit me tonight in a way that it hadn't before. Perhaps it was a college acceptance letter he received this afternoon and that gnawing sensation that he'll be leaving the house shortly. I won't even count the months he has left; suffice it to say it's probably around eight or nine.

"You look so handsome tonight," I told him. "Thanks," he smiled, a bit embarrassed, I think. I mean, seriously, who likes to hear that from their mom?! And then off he drove with my husband to his destination.

A few moments later, a text came through from my younger son telling me that he, too, was off to a friend's house but would be home in time for dinner.

Tears and then more tears. How did I get here? I know, I know. It's a rhetorical question. It's been 19 years since we welcomed our first child into our lives, and they have been both wonderful and challenging years. The thousands of individual moments that go into parenting, the not knowing if we are making the "right" choices, the "right" decisions, the "right" everything. For so long, it was a waiting game, a hoping game. Was I too harsh with that consequence? Should I have encouraged her to read more? Why didn't I push him to play travel soccer? Did I spend enough time with each of them individually? How did I miss the stress building up inside of them? Was I present enough, loving enough, tough enough, gentle enough? The questions never cease; the second-guessing has become a low-grade sound frequency that has become part of the music of my psyche.

And then, a crescendo burst on the scene, allowing me to see that I have raised good kids—decent, kind, thoughtful, respectful, imperfect kids.

They don't know it, but I pray for them every day, for their safety, well-being, health, and happiness. Even before I get out of bed in the morning, I ask God to watch over them and protect them. I pray for them to feel a sense of wholeness and inner peace in the midst of their teenage angst-filled years.

Looking at the words of this prayer, the wishes—"Grant peace, well-being and blessing, grace, love, and mercy for us"—are the same ones I wish for my children.* May they be blessed with goodness and blessing, grace, loving-kindness, and mercy.

While my wish is for them to be blessed with those traits, my other deep wish is for them to bless the world with goodness, blessing, grace, loving-kindness, and mercy. By coaching them to embody these qualities and seeing each of them truly live these values, I know that one aspect of my job as mom has been accomplished.

ג

*V-tov b-einechah, l-vahraych et amcha Yisrael
b-chol ayt oo-v-chol shah'ah, bi-sh'lomechah.*

May it please You to bless Your people Israel,
at all times and in each hour with Your peace.

Raising two young boys close in age was very challenging because they were extremely energetic. My two sons did not leave each other alone. Having grown up with a much younger brother, I was unaware of the dynamics of two brothers; that is, until I had two boys. I swear the two of them were like lion cubs, always wrestling and jumping all over one another. My wise daughter learned how to stay away from them as they rumbled and tumbled. For nearly 15 years, all I wished for was peace between them. Instead, I tended cuts and other "accidents" they inflicted upon one another. Like that time when my five-year-old threw a book into his seven-year-old brother's cheek; he still has the scar to prove it. Or the time when they were seriously wrestling and I had to break up the fight (I knew they might clobber each other, but I was pretty sure they

---

*And if truth be told, I wish these qualities for every human being on our planet. It's easy to wish these values for those who are near and dear to us and much harder to wish them for strangers. *Sim Shalom*'s universal nature reminds me that we are all in this human endeavor together.

wouldn't clobber me!).

Several years later, when my boys were about eight and ten, I remember bumping into a family friend in the grocery store and asking her if there was any hope for my boys becoming friends. She relayed that her boys couldn't stand each other growing up; they fought all the time. Now, they are the best of friends. Chuckling to myself, I thought, "Yeah, that will never happen in my house."

When my boys were in eleventh and ninth grade, respectively, they started to attend the same high school. With a busy summer, I had little time to prepare—physically, mentally, or emotionally—for the upcoming school year. As I sent my ninth grader off for two days of orientation, my youngest daughter asked me, "Mom, is it weird that you now have two high schoolers?" Dismissing the question, I abruptly answered, "I think I'm in denial."

6:30 Monday morning arrived much too early. As I turned off my alarm clock, it was time to make sure everyone else was awake, time to pack lunches, and time to get breakfast ready. A mad dash out the door at 7:20 and we were off, but not before the obligatory first day of school photos. Thank goodness, they still humor me and give me that pleasure!

Despite the orientation of the last week, I knew my middle son was nervous. Before we pulled out of the driveway, I sent a quick text to my oldest, sitting in the back seat, saying, "Please keep this quiet… I think your brother is nervous about his first day. Please be kind and maybe say something to help him feel more comfortable?" While I wasn't sure that he would respond, or how he would receive the text, I felt that it was worth sending. Even if the physical roughhousing had diminished over the years, there still existed a "healthy competition" between the two of them, which included much "trash talk" to one another.

To my utter surprise, as I rarely get a response to the texts I send, I hear from my eldest, Yossi, "Mom, I got it." I smiled in return, curious to see how he would handle this early morning request. Once we began driving to their school, he started asking his younger brother questions and cracking some jokes so that my ninth grader was actually laughing. As I pulled up to drop them off, I wished them both a great day and then turned to see them walking together, side by side. I heard Yossi ask Eitan if he knew where he was going for his first class; Eitan responded, well actually grunted, "yeah." It was a true "big brother" moment and my heart could not have been fuller!

> ...*V-tov b-einechah, l-vahraych et amcha Yisrael*
> *b-chol ayt oo–v–chol shah'ah, bi-sh'lomechah.*

May it please You to bless Your people Israel,
at all times and in each hour with Your peace.

Was this a moment of blessing that I was witnessing? Here were two sons of Yisrael, who had struggled for so many years. The name Yisrael was actually given to Jacob in the book of Genesis after he wrestled with his brother, Esau.* Delving into the word *yisra-el,* one will find the word—*sar*—which means to wrestle. Both of these Biblical and modern Israelites spent plenty of years wrestling with one another.

As I watched my boys walk away into the distance together, I was overcome with emotion "Wow. It happened. It actually happened. Peace between two brothers!" Could it actually be possible that they would be *"blessed with peace in every season and at all times"*? Okay, okay, I know that's pushing it; the "in every season and at all times" part probably won't happen in the near future, but I'm so grateful to God for the now. Grateful for the privilege of having raised them this far, I was struck at the passage of time and growth, both physical and emotional. I had a quick flash forward to a day when I will no longer be on Planet Earth and was comforted by the support and love I saw between my two boys. It has been a long road to get to this point and I remain incredibly thankful to have witnessed it.

---

*Genesis 32:29: "...Your name shall no longer be Jacob, but Israel, for you have striven with beings divine and human, and have prevailed."

Ways to Promote Peace

1) Be kind, always.

2) Choose words carefully.

3) Appreciate differences by attending various cultural and/or religious fairs and institutions.

4) Attend multi-ethnic events, such as concerts, art shows, or dance performances.

5) Read books about peace and discuss how to bring more peace into your family, community, and world.

6) Encourage and support your children to have a diverse group of friends.

Peace: Questions to Consider

1) What does peace mean to you?

2) Is peace just the absence of war?

3) Jewish tradition teaches that the root for peace, shalom, is shalem, meaning whole or complete. How could this notion expand your current understanding of peace?

4) In what ways do you work for peace in your personal life? Your family? Your community? The world?

Trust

(Ein Camocha)

א

Ein camocha ba'Elohim, Adonai, v'ein c'ma'asecha.

There is none like you, O God, none like Your deeds.

One night on the way home from jiu jitsu, two of my children and I were patiently waiting for the red arrow to turn green in the left-hand turn lane. As the light changed, I lifted my foot off of the brake, getting ready to accelerate; suddenly, the car in front of me stalled, so I quickly placed my foot back on the brake. At that moment, we all felt a huge impact as the car behind me crashed into us. With my kids screaming in the background, my first response was, naturally, to make sure everyone was OK.

After I heard both of their sweet voices, my son said, "Mom, I'm coming up front, there is glass everywhere." We pulled over to the side and luckily the guy in the car that hit me pulled over as well. Once I got out of the car and saw the damage, I freaked out. Fortunately, we had a bike hitch on the back, as my son was seated in the last row of our minivan and it was the bike rack that absorbed most of the impact. The entire back window had been shattered and the glass had flown all over the back of my minivan. Thank God, no one got a scratch.

Noticing this miracle, that not one of us had been injured, my 10-year-old said, "Mom, we are lucky that we have our angels to protect us." "Yes, indeed," I acknowledged, "and be sure to thank them."

As I spoke with the other guy, trying to calm him down after he saw my children emerge from the car, my son came over to me and asked, "Mom, do you think Albert Einstein is my guardian angel?"

"Eitan, I don't know," and went back to getting the insurance information that I needed to file a claim.

A few seconds later, Eitan came back and asked again, "But Mom, do you think that Albert Einstein is my guardian angel?"

Again, "Eitan, I don't know."

Obviously not satisfied with my answer, Eitan asked for a third time, "Mom! Do you think Albert Einstein is my guardian angel?"

Exasperated, I exclaimed, "Eitan, if you want him to be your guardian angel, then yes, he's your guardian angel, but I'm a bit busy right now, so please stop asking me this question."

A few minutes later, my husband arrived to take the kids home; I waited to finish up with the police and then finally went home.

Early the next morning, I was at home taking care of some things on the computer. I went to check my email and found something strange in my inbox. The return address was from QuotesofEncouragment@trunk-consequence.com, not an address I recognized. With my curiosity piqued, I clicked on it and found only one line, which read, "There are only two ways to live your life. One is as though nothing is a miracle. The other is as though everything is a miracle." Albert Einstein.

WHOA!! That was just really bizarre. After my son's continual prompting about Albert Einstein being his guardian angel, this was just a bit freaky. Needing to find a rational answer, I called my husband and thanked him for sending me the email.

"Nope, wasn't me," he said.

I texted the only other friend who knew about the accident and thanked her for the quote.

"Sorry, wasn't me," she replied.

Hmm...I sent back a reply thanking the person who sent it for their words and asked them to identify themselves. No response there, either.

To this day, I have no idea who sent that email, nor how it got to me, nor the strange return address mentioning the "trunk consequence."

When my son came home from school that day, I told him what had transpired. He smiled and said, "That is just really freaky, Mom."

Yes, I agree, it is really freaky and definitely gives me pause to think about a bigger picture. Sharing this idea with my son, admitting that there is a Mystery out there that we don't understand, and discussing these ideas with my children, I believe provided them with a level of comfort around the Unknown. As my children grow in their own lives, and encounter events they may not understand, I hope that they will be more comfortable living in the Mystery and the **not** knowing. My prayer is that even in the lack of clarity, they will have the inner fortitude to weather life's challenging times. Helping give my kids language to discuss life's Mystery provides them the ability to tap into the Divine as they work to overcome their struggles.

I guess there are some who could say that I randomly received this email, but how likely is it that the quote would be from Albert Einstein? There are thousands of famous people who have shared meaningful and inspiring words. On top of that, why was my son hounding me about Albert Einstein being his guardian angel only 15 hours prior to my receiving this email? So, what did I take away from this experience? Trust and gratitude. For years, I have been working on trusting God and found some solace in the beginning of this *Ein Camocha* prayer.

The opening words, *"Ein camocha ba-elohim, Adonai, v'ein c'ma'asecha."* There is none like you, God, and there is nothing like your deeds. I do believe that it was God (and an entourage of angels) that kept us safe during the car accident. As crazy as it may sound, it seems the most logical explanation to me.* The car behind me had to be travelling at least 20 mph to do the damage that was done—the window completely shattered, glass strewn throughout the car—and yet we all walked away unscathed. And then, of course, there is that question from my son mixed up with the email of unknown origin. When I reflect on the words of this prayer, I can truly say that there is none like God and nothing like God's actions. I continue to learn to trust in God.

In our very science-oriented society, trusting in something that we can neither see nor touch is not so easily understood or accepted. I am sure

---

*I recognize that this thought implies that God was there to protect us, which would have to mean that when someone gets hurt, God is not there to protect them. I am troubled by this and do not believe that God does harm to humans. As my own theology emerges, I have come to learn that we have two kinds of theologies: operative and espoused. Espoused theology is the theology we intellectually believe in; operative theology is the theology from which we operate, how it informs what we actually do. Often times they are in direct conflict. While my espoused theology does not believe that God causes harm, my operative theology feels that God did protect us. I know these beliefs are in opposition and that it doesn't make much sense, but I am working on and learning to live with what it means to hold two diametrically opposite views as true.

there are those who might think, well, if God really wanted to protect you, why didn't He prevent the car accident in the first place? I don't believe that God caused the accident; I believe that the careless driver behind me caused the accident. What I do believe is that God is present with us, during difficult times, protecting and guiding us. It is in this notion that I have learned to trust. Trust that no matter what life brings, I can depend on God to help me get through the challenges and difficulties that will come my way.

How, you may ask, does God help us get through the trying times? The secret can be found in the juxtaposition of God's names in this prayer. We read two names for God in the first sentence: *Elohim* and *Adonai*. Why are two different names needed? A literal translation would be, "There is none like you, God, God." Why the repetition of God's name? In Jewish tradition, each name of God has a unique meaning. The meaning related to the name *Elohim* relates to God's aspect of judgment, while the meaning related to *Adonai* relates to God's aspect of mercy. It is in the balancing of these two that our trust in God lies. Just as a parent knows when to use judgment toward her child and when to use mercy, so too, does God. Through the use of both names of God, we can come to trust that God supports us through judgment and mercy. While there will be many events that transpire in our lives for which we are unable to provide a rational explanation, we always have the ability to reach out to God to provide us guidance and support. Ultimately, we understand that living life involves many unknowns and that there is a powerful force in the Universe, rooting for us and beckoning us with judgment and mercy.

בּ

Adonai melech, Adonai malach, Adonai yimloch l'olam va'ed.

Adonai rules, Adonai has ruled, Adonai will rule forever.

One day on the way home from synagogue, my son took out a packet of Hanukkah gelt from his pocket to eat. Now, that wouldn't normally raise any eyebrows except that it was February. I asked him where he got it from and he then proceeded to pull out three more packets. He told me that he "found" them by the synagogue kitchen, and that since no one had eaten them in two months, he thought he would eat them. I asked him if he had gotten permission from the kitchen ladies and he replied, "No." Needless to say, I was not happy. I explained to him that while no one had eaten them in two months, they did not belong to him and taking them was, in essence, stealing. He continued to offer up myriad reasons why it was okay to take them. I rebutted with myriad reasons why it was **not** okay. I then let him know that he would need to return the unopened packets and that he would have to pay for the packet he had eaten. The following week, he left one dollar for the *kiddush* ladies and explained to them what had happened. As anticipated, they responded with love and smiles; the following Shabbat, they served the remaining chocolate gelt for kiddush.

After the event transpired, one of the *kiddush* ladies came over to me and said, "You didn't have to have your son pay for the candy." I replied, "Yes, I did. It wasn't so much for what he took, but rather for the fact that it was sneaky."

For me, the issue was about trust. While the item was small and the act relatively harmless, it was the larger lesson that I wanted him to learn: "Even when no one is looking, you need to be honest. I need to be able to trust you." Over the years, I have felt like a broken record telling my kids the importance of being honest. I'm sure they will tell you what we tell them regularly, "It's very easy to lose our trust, and very hard to gain it back."

For me, being trustworthy is one of the universal principles that is non-negotiable—it is past, present, and future... forever. Being trustworthy is one value that does not change, even though circumstances might. Like God, it is Eternal. We read in this prayer that God has ruled in the past, rules in the present, and will rule in the future. God's ruling and God's rule are forever. For me, being trustworthy mirrors this notion of past, present, and future. Consequently, when I was told that my son didn't have to pay for the candy, for me that was non-negotiable: I am working to raise children who are trustworthy—always. Should I have let him off the hook? Maybe... Was I too harsh in my response? Perhaps... but if truth be told, I was probably responding to my own childhood dishonesty that was buried deep inside.

I remember being about 10 years old and going to my elementary school's Mother's Day Gift Boutique. There was an adorable "pompom pet." I remember the details to this day: It was a cute little elephant made from brown pompoms, dressed in green clothing, with big felt ears and googly eyes. It was so cute and I wanted to give it to my mom but didn't have 50 cents to buy it. While I was standing around admiring it, my "friends" were encouraging me to steal it. Feeling sucked into the peer pressure, I acquiesced, and when the parent volunteers looked away, I quickly tucked this little pet into my pocket. I remember feeling quite proud of myself as we all left the boutique. That pride lasted for all of a few seconds until I started to feel a sickening feeling deep in the pit of my stomach. I wanted to return it and apologize, but I was too busy receiving praise from my friends.

As the days passed, I felt worse and worse and didn't feel comfortable sharing what I had done with anyone, least of all my parents. My conscience had gotten the better of me and I felt totally trapped. "Think, Amy, think…" My mind created endless scenarios: I could walk back into the boutique and just place the elephant on the table, or I could just throw it away, not give it to my mom as a gift, thereby receiving no benefit from my stealing.

The days turned into weeks and now I had no hope of returning the gift. I needed a gift for Mother's Day, so I broke down and gave her the pompom pet. The guilt I felt was torturous. Finally, one night, while watching my mom handle some PTA monies, I came up with a brilliant idea! I would take the 50 cents that I owed for the pet and sneakily add it to her existing school funds. And that is just what I did. I would wind up paying for it, although it was not until many years later that I ever divulged this story to her.

Even at 10, I intuitively knew that stealing did not feel good, so perhaps it was my inner 10-year-old jumping out and insisting that my son pay for those chocolates. It was a lesson that I learned early on; now, as an adult raising trustworthy children, it has become an important value for me. I want my children to be trustworthy always—past, present, future. And while this is my core belief, I'm not naïve enough to believe that they will always be trustworthy. They will no doubt have their own "pompom pet" moments, and all I can do is hope that they, too, will learn from them and ultimately strive to be trustworthy adults.

ג

ki v'cha l'vad batachnu

For in You alone do we place our trust.

Read the front page of a newspaper, turn on the TV, click on Yahoo's homepage, and there before your very eyes will be a barrage of treacherous events. There are so many disheartening events occurring daily around the world. Taking in all of this information on a regular basis has made it hard for me not to worry. I have spent many a sleepless night worrying about the safety of my children. From the macro to the micro, I have every kind of worry. What kind of world will they grow up in? How much environmental damage are we doing to the planet? Will they grow up healthy? Will I live long enough to be a grandma? Will my children become successful adults? Will they be able to support themselves? The list goes on and on.

Several years ago, my husband bought me a book called *The Worrywart's Companion*. At the time, it was cute and I did flip through it, but even then I felt as if no book could help me overcome my compulsive worrying. I was forever looking for the "magic bullet" that would alleviate my worrying. And then it happened. I was standing in services one Shabbat morning and the words from this prayer jumped out at me: *ki v'cha l'vad batachnu*, For in You alone do we trust. My mind flashed through the various centuries of Jewish history and all that the Jewish people have experienced. Yet these words endure, seared in our prayer book: "For in You alone do we trust." How can we possibly trust in a God who seems to act less and less in history? The God who split the Sea of Reeds and appeared at Sinai with thunder and lightning does not seem to be stopping tsunamis and hurricanes, wars or warlords?

As one of my children said to me in passing, "Everything involves a risk." Yes, everything does involve a risk: driving to work, running an errand, going on vacation, walking the dog—but the question remains, how do we live with that knowledge? We can become hermits and never leave our homes (and then of course, a tree could fall on our home!), or we can move into a place of trust. While I move in and out of this space, after our car accident and the email from God-knows-who, I have been reminded that my work to trust God continues.

My effort to connect to this trust is continual, as it is my nature to worry despite my valiant attempts not to. How do I know my kids will turn out ok? How do I know that the way I'm raising them is the "right" way? How do I know that they will grow into successful adults? How do I know that they will be free from harm's way? The cold, hard truth is that I don't and I won't. These questions and many others have kept me up many a night and have distracted me from much work. So how do I move forward with my life?

I have learned to live as much as I can in the moment. I have also come to accept and believe that I am doing the best I can. As one of my dear friends says on a regular basis, "I may not be doing everything 'right' but I give myself an 'A+' for effort." This thinking has kept me from continuing to beat myself up for not doing more, not doing things better and faster. While it is hard at times for me to make decisions, I have learned, by noticing my feelings, to trust my intuition. Before I make a decision, I check in with myself to see if it feels "right"; if the answer is yes, I proceed. If the answer is no, I'll reassess. For me, learning to trust my intuition really comes down to connecting to that piece of Divinity that is in me—my soul, and my spirit. For in **You** do we place our trust—**You** as Divine Life Force and **You** as the piece of **You** that is part of me.

I am working on learning to trust both of these notions— my intuition and the Universal Life Force that runs through creation. I do not know what will be with my children, but I do know and trust that there is a greater force at work, moving and reaching out in a multiplicity of directions. And I do know that while there are no guarantees of what life will bring me, I trust that I have the know-how to weather whatever storms may come my way. I trust that I have a wonderful family, an incredible group of friends, a warm and loving community, and many caring acquaintances who will be there when I need support, be it in times of joy or times of sorrow.

I trust that in **You** I see myself reflected as part of the greater whole, and I trust that my ability to connect to the **You** inside me will enable me to move forward—in my life and in raising my children—with much meaning, much joy, and much gratitude.

Ways to Garner Trust

1) Begin each day with an affirmative statement, "I trust in a Higher Power that all will go well."
2) Review situations in your life that worked out for the best (although they didn't seem that way initially).
3) Do something that takes you out of your comfort zone (e.g., hang gliding, parasailing, trapeze school, scuba diving).
4) Blindfold: Blindfold one person and have the other one hold their hand and walk them around, being sure to describe the environment.
5) Trust Fall: In pairs of similar size, one becomes a Faller and one the Catcher. Teach methods for spotting, falling, and catching. Start small and build to bigger falls, then swap. Debrief. What made you feel more or less trusting?
6) Find a mantra that works for you and use it when you are in difficult situations. You can try the words from this prayer, "*Ein Camocha Ba'Elohim, Ado-nai* or "*ki v'cha l'vad batachnu.*" Some other suggestions: "In You I trust," or just repeating the word trust: *bitachon* (בטחון), security."

Trust: Questions to Consider

1) Why is trust an important value?
2) What might be some ways to model and teach trust to your children?
3) How does trust or a lack of trust inform your relationships?
4) Are you able to trust in a Higher Power? Why or why not?

Learning
(Eitz Chayim)

א

Eitz chayim hee
lah-mahchahzeekeem bah
v-tomchehah m'ushar.

She is a tree of life
to those who hold fast to her;
and all of her supporters are happy.

Oh, what I wouldn't do right now to be a Mama Tree, with my children following my every instruction and doing so enthusiastically—which would inevitably lead to their happiness (insert sarcasm here). I think back to the days when my daughter would wrap her arms around my legs as she walked next to me. Feeling encumbered at the time, I would give anything to go back to those sweet days when "Mom" was someone you wanted to hold onto. Even as my children grew and turned five, eight, and 10, they were still clinging... but now as 13-, 15-, and 17-year-olds, not a chance in hell—or so I thought.

The words of the *Eitz Chayim* prayer are sung to the Torah herself, at the end of the Torah service. Acknowledging the many lessons and teachings that we can glean from her, we sing goodbye and return her to the ark.

But what is the meaning behind those words, "She is a tree of life to those who hold fast to her, and all of her supporters are happy." Is this true? I'm sure you know people who study Torah and are not happy; however, I believe that the premise of this prayer intimates that through studying, learning, and living Torah, one has the ability to move in the direction of joy and happiness.

Perhaps this stems from a deep-seated belief that when done well, the power of learning is transformative and life-giving.

Jews are often referred to as "people of the book," and a disproportionate number of Jews have higher level degrees in comparison to our demographic numbers. Education is a central component of our Jewish values. Throughout history, when the Jews were expelled from various countries, they were not allowed to take any possessions; yet, what they could take were their brains—their education, their learning.

While the *Eitz Chayim* prayer specifically refers to the Torah scroll—the Five Books of Moses—which is being returned to the ark, I like the teaching that Torah can be a much broader term.* The word Torah has as its root the Hebrew letters הרה, meaning "teaching," and so the word "Torah" can refer to the written Torah, the oral Torah, the Talmud, the Midrash, or the various other Jewish books that have been written throughout the ages. In more modern parlance, *Torah* can be each person's own teachings, their own truths. One might say to another, "What's your Torah?" meaning, what are your eternal truths, what do you want to teach the world?

Of course, as a mom, I think that I have lots of *Torah* to teach. What parent doesn't? The only problem is that now with teenagers, my kids are not always so ready to hear my words of wisdom, my gleanings, my teachings, my eternal truths. In fact, I often get the sense that they tune me out. So often, I feel like I'm talking to a brick wall. I wonder to myself, "Do they hear me?" Most of the time, the answer is no—but mainly due to the headphones that they incessantly wear. It took me several months to realize that when I don't get an answer after yelling three or four times, chances are they are not listening—or more accurately, they are not hearing.

So you can imagine my surprise when, talking to my 17-year-old about girls, he actually admitted that he cared what I had to say. Wow! Well, it wasn't expressed that clearly; in fact, it was more like incomplete phrases. When I told him that he was going to do what he wanted anyway, and so I was just going to keep my mouth shut, he responded with, "I actually do care... I mean I'm okay with... I know I don't always seem like it... but I do care what you have to say... as long as it doesn't have to do with religion."

I was in shock!! These words from a kid who does not always share

---

*Thanks to my teacher Reb Daniel Siegel who pointed out to me that while in the service these words are referring to the Torah, in their original source, the book of Proverbs 3:18, the words are referring to Wisdom, Herself, which in essence means that everyone has their own Torah/wisdom.

information so readily and often appears not to be listening to me. But alas, I guess he listens and hears a lot more than he lets on. And while I certainly would not deem that response "a clinging moment," it did shift my consciousness, leading me to an important realization: Even if my children do not appear to be listening, I should continue to talk—to speak my truths, teach my values, and offer my guidance—because there is ultimately still a little boy or girl inside those big teenagers. And sometimes, on rare occasions, we catch a glimpse of their little hands reaching out to grasp their Mama Tree.

ב

Kee lekach tov, nahtati lachem, Toratee al tah'ahzovu.

A precious teaching I gave you, do not forsake my Torah.

I didn't quite know how to respond when my son told me that he and his girlfriend broke up. They had been together several months, which of course feels much longer when you are in high school. She was a great girl: kind, respectful, smart, athletic, cultured, funny, generous, and interesting. She had been to our house many times and we all liked her very much. So, when I heard the news, I wanted to be supportive of my son; yet I wasn't sure how much to comfort, how much to question, and how much to just remain silent.

What I really wanted to say was, "So what did you learn from this relationship? What qualities did you like in her that you'd look for again the next time? What worked? What didn't? What would you have done differently? How were you as a partner? as well as a dozen or so other questions. Thank God, I erred on the side of silence plus a few comforting words, letting him know I was available if he wanted to talk.

A few weeks later, I noticed another girl's name being mentioned. Hmmm...interesting...I thought he really cared about his ex-girlfriend, so what's going on with this new girl? A few more days passed and I asked him who this new girl was?

"Oh, she's in one of my classes."

"Do you like her?

"Yeah, she's nice."

"I thought you and Sami* just broke up?"

"Yeah, we did."

"And I thought you were upset?"

"Yeah, I was."

"So, why are you going to date someone else? It's only been a couple of weeks. Why don't you take some time to think about things and just be on your own for a while?"

Silence.

"You know when you date someone right after a breakup, things usually don't work out. It's called being on the rebound."

Silence.

"Did you hear me?

"Yeah."

I knew right then that the conversation was over and that it was better not to continue my monologue. I didn't bring the subject up again, but I noticed the frequency with which my son was talking to the new girl, and then they started hanging out. Once again, I tried to broach the subject and explain the meaning of "being on the rebound," realizing that no one was listening. I decided to speak to the only one who was listening—me! "OK, I get it—he needs to learn this one on his own, by experience. Let it go, Amy."

More time passed and then the two of them were "dating." Painstakingly, I continued to hold my tongue and unhappily made myself available to carpool them when needed. Seeing your children make mistakes (in your opinion) is not easy, nor is parenting teenagers. Several weeks passed and the school year was almost over. My son and I happened to be in the car together when he piped up with the following: "You know, I've been thinking about some stuff, and I have some ideas about the qualities that I'd like my next girlfriend to have."

Did I actually hear that correctly? Wow, had he really been thinking about his past relationship in contrast to his current one? Trying not to respond overzealously, I calmly inquired, "Can you say more about that?"

---

*All names have been changed for privacy.

"Yeah, for sure. I learned that I need someone who is affectionate, gives compliments and makes me feel good about myself, and is a positive influence on me to help me make the right decisions. And she needs to be smart. I mean, you can only talk about superficial things for so long, no matter how good-looking she is."

I was literally jumping for joy and did my best to remain calm, cool, and collected. "Oh, that's interesting. I agree that those are important traits, and while it's important for you to feel good about yourself without someone telling you this, it is nice to have a supportive partner."

Slowly piecing things together, I was trying to discern how he reached this conclusion, and I was getting a clearer picture. Regardless, what I was most pleased with was his thinking about these relationships and learning from them.

From the time my children were young, I have repeatedly asked them the same question, "What can you learn from this?" It doesn't matter the situation at hand—conflicts with friends or family, difficult experiences, challenging encounters—they all receive the same question: "What's your takeaway? What can you learn from this?"

It is interesting to note that the Hebrew root of the word Torah is the same Hebrew root for the word parent: *horeh* (הרה), to instruct. While the Torah is the Jewish people's instruction manual, passed down to us over the millennia, perhaps our personal Torah can be understood as the wisdom we use to parent our children.

I like to think of the Torah as a guidebook—a map that helps me navigate the challenges of our world. In it are trials and tribulations of what worked and what didn't work, stories about family dynamics and communal relationships. Each time we return the Torah to the ark, we recite this prayer that reminds us of the valuable lessons we can find in Her:

Ki lekach tov, natati lachem, Torati al ta'azovu.
A precious teaching I give you, never leave my Torah.

When I recite these words, I am reminded of my own prayer, the prayer that my son has learned from my Torah ("What can you learn from this?"), and reminded that he will continue to create his own Torah and share it with the world.

ג

Hahsheeveinu Adonai aylechah v-nahshuvah
chahdaysh yahmeinu k-kedem.

Help us to return to You, and we shall return.
Renew our days as You did before.

I could hear it in her voice. I knew she was going to burst into tears when she arrived home. My daughter had been at sleepaway camp for seven weeks, and after our brief conversation as she headed to the airport for her flight home, I could just tell she needed a good cry. My intuition told me that she had been holding it together for so long and needed a safe place to download and unload all that she had carried during these weeks away.

Sure, she had great friends, amazing counselors, and a supportive staff, but sometimes there are things that you just can't say freely without fear of judgment—to anyone, except to your mom. Yes, we have our spats and disagreements, but I'm so grateful and feel very lucky that my teenage daughter still wants to talk to me. When I heard her cheerful, tired voice, I sensed, somehow, that she needed a good cry.

After a three-hour delay from a terrible storm, the four of us drove out at 11:00 p.m. to pick her up from the airport. How wonderful it was to see her! Despite having been up since 5 a.m., she was upbeat, happy, and very talkative. Hmm... maybe I misjudged... maybe I've been away from her so long that I was wrong and she is just fine. We grabbed her drenched luggage, loaded it in the car, and headed home. Arriving home close to midnight, I was exhausted and was ready to head to bed.

"Goodnight, I'm so happy to have you home." As I looked up to go hug her, she had that look in her eye and the lower lip quiver... and then the floodgates opened. Tears streaming down her cheeks, nose running, words outpouring, "I just want to be back at camp. I thought I wanted to be home, in my bed, in my room, but now that I'm here I realize that I just want to be back in my bunk, sleeping with my friends and counselors in a dirty bed with a gross bathroom. I couldn't wait to come home, and now that I'm back, I just want camp..." The words continued to flow—about friends and experiences, about things she learned and things she had to keep inside—and now she was free and safe to let it all go.

I hugged her. I kissed her. I patted her head. I listened. There was so much I wanted to say, and I knew that in that moment, there was nothing to say. I validated her emotions and tried to normalize her feelings, but ultimately, it was one of the moments when all one can do is be present for another's pain and sorrow.

As the tears continued, I reflected back to my own return home from summer camp, and I knew just how she felt. The fun of camp, the close friendships, the growth and challenges, the pushing of one's boundaries, the laughter and the pure joy of being in nature—all of it came rushing back. In that moment, I wished that I, too, could go back in time and return to those magical days filled with wonder and fun!

Hahsheeveinu Adonai aylechah v-nahshuvah
chahdaysh yahmeinu k-kedem.

Help us to return to You, and we shall return.
Renew our days as You did before.

Oh, to be a camper again and enjoy the simplicity of life. Hiking the Appalachian Trail; white water rafting on the Delaware River; stargazing from the boys' campus; learning new skills and exploring unknown talents; the nostalgia came flooding in. Oh, how I wish I could return to those days of old.

chahdaysh yahmeinu k-kedem.
Renew our days as you did before.

Each time I hear this verse recited, I am taken back to my younger self, the one without all of the responsibilities, the one who didn't realize at the time how good she had it. I'm really happy with my life. I love my family, friends, and community; still, there is that little girl hidden deep inside who just wishes she could play all day long, jumping in puddles, watching frogs in the morning light, taking it all in and yet not even realizing the pure magnificence of the moment.

I've been reciting these words for many years, and the older I get, the more meaningful they become. These words trigger not just my desire to go back to the days of the past, but also my desire to move ahead toward the future. Reciting them provides me with the insight that I can turn to when I've lost my way.

Hahsheeveinu Adonai aylechah v-nahshuvah
chahdaysh yahmeinu k-kedem.

Help us to return to You, and we shall return.
Renew our days as You did before.

Each time we return the Torah to the ark, we speak to the possibility of finding wisdom in the Torah, the Divine Guidebook that was handed down to the Jewish people thousands of years ago. Through these words, we ask for help in turning, so that we may return.

Over the years, I have come to understand this line in different ways. The one that currently holds the most meaning for me relates to the notion of "stuckness." Sometimes we are just stuck; we get in our own way. We see things from only one perspective—ours! We don't want to hear from others; we don't want advice. We want to do things OUR way. And then one day, we might wake up and realize that our life is not what we had imagined or desired. How do we get out of the rut? We begin by realizing that we need to shift. We need a new direction.

By asking the Holy One of Blessing for help, we can return, albeit slowly, to our true selves. In my understanding, this return to our true selves is a metaphorical call to go back to or reconnect to our souls, to our essence. Jewish mystical tradition teaches that when Adam and Eve were in the Garden of Eden, they were completely connected to the Divine. Their expulsion from the garden (for eating from the tree of knowledge of good and evil, the one God told them not to eat from) was not a "punishment" in the way that we think. Rather, it was a consequence of their coming to understand duality in our world. This false sense of being cut off from God and being cut off from their true essence is the hidden secret to this story and is what was passed down to us as their progeny. When we recite these words,

Hahsheeveinu Adonai aylechah v-nahshuvah
chahdeish yahmeinu k-kedem.

Help us to return to You, and we shall return.
Renew our days as You did before.

what we are really asking for is a return to our true Essence, to that place of Divine connection and unity. Most times we forget this truth. My summers at camp that I remember so fondly were so precious precisely because it was there that I felt deeply connected to the Source of All. It was there where I felt my truest, most authentic sense of self.

In my heart of hearts, I know that is what my daughter also felt. There is a certain *je ne sais quoi* that comes from living simply, from being unplugged and disconnected from technology and fiercely connected to the pulse of life that runs through a magical summer camp experience. That sense of connection is true wisdom, and that is precisely what the Torah teaches us as we return her gently to the ark. May we each have a sweet returning to Deep Connection and Knowing.

Ways to Facilitate Learning

1) Go outside more often and explore nature's beauty.
Try to find an orchard or strawberry patch
nearby and go pick some fruit.
2) Use the world as a classroom, seeing how and what we
can learn from every person and every experience.
3) Learn how a Torah is written. If possible, take
a field trip to meet a local *sofer* (scribe).
4) Try as often as possible to have family dinners that include
"thinking questions," such as, "How did you exhibit bravery
today? Kindness? Failure? Share something new that you learned
today." Parents and kids should both participate. It's important
for kids to hear about their parents' growth and struggles.
5) Create a family Torah scroll. Take two branches and
some paper to wrap around them. Design a beautiful
cover. Have each family member write down their
"Torah." Revisit this document, adding to this every
couple of years as each person's Torah evolves.

Learning: Questions to Consider

1) How do you keep the lines of communication
open with your children?
2) Do you share your Torah (*aka*, your core
values) with your children regularly?
3) How might you discuss with your children the
lessons that are available for learning in events that
have both negative and positive outcomes?
4) What are the special places that allow you to feel
"held and safe"? Have each family member identify
their modern day *Gan Eden* (Garden of Eden).
5) How can you connect more deeply to your family?
How can you help your children do the same?

Boundaries

(Kaddish)

א

Yitgahdahl v-yitkahdash sh'may rahbah
b-ahlmah divrah chir'ootayv-yahmleech mahlchootay

Let the glory of God be extolled.
Let God's great name be hallowed,
in the world whose creation Adonai willed.
May God's sovereignty soon prevail.

I was talking with my daughter, relaxing on her bed, when she said, "Mom, I have to tell you something but I don't want you to be upset." I could only imagine what was about to come out of my preteen daughter's mouth. Did she have another fight with her best friend and do something horrible? Did she fail a test in school? Did she lose a valuable item? My mind was racing; I couldn't imagine what I was about to hear.

"Mom, I know that I'm your baby and that you don't like for me to grow up, but I'm twelve now and it's time that I need to do something.

"Just tell me already!" I wanted to scream.

"I've been thinking, Mom…and I don't want to hurt your feelings, but I'm growing up and I want to change my room. Just listen—don't respond until I finish," she pleaded.

"I want to repaint, get new furniture, get a rug, replace my laundry basket, and I really, really want to get rid of the wallpaper border. Oh and by the way, I've already researched on Amazon what I want to buy and how much it will cost. So can I buy it?"

I sat quietly, listening, truly impressed with her presentation, but secretly mourning. All I could focus on was that she hated the border with those sweet, multi-colored, whimsical fairies with wings and flowers. The one I painstakingly selected after looking through a multitude of choices. I couldn't even process the rest of what she was saying as I was imagining her room fairy-free.

"Well, can I do it? Can I? Can I show you what I want? Can I order it now?"

All of my daughter's incessant questions quickly brought me back to my current reality. My daughter was growing up and I had to deal with it—and quick!

We then proceeded to talk about each item, what she would keep, what we would think about replacing, but one thing was non-negotiable: The fairies had to go.

Over the years, my teenage children have drawn new boundaries and crossed over many thresholds related to space, time, and relationships. One day, my son had his girlfriend over, and I walked into his room to ask him a question, only to find her in his bed, under his covers lying next to him. (Yes, they were fully clothed and yes the door was open but, really?) They were immediately asked to find public space to spend the rest of their time together.

When my sons started going through puberty, I knew it would be weird, but I have to be honest, it was much more awkward than I antici-pated. We all experienced great discomfort with their changing bodies. Although being the Mom of two boys who shave does feel a bit strange, it makes me smile now when I look over old family photos of my boys as toddlers, faces covered with shaving cream, "shaving" with their dad and their grandfather.

I never could have imagined any of these situations until they crept into my current reality. When I bathed my babies, wiped their noses, changed their diapers, fed them meals, I rarely stopped to fast-forward to what it would be like when they turned into teenagers. Now, routinely, doors are locked, even amidst the request for them to remain open. While we still eat meals together, everyone decides what their palate prefers. It is not easy watching them grow up. Boundaries about how much to say, what to say, if to say, how much to do, what to do, if to do, are forefront in my mind.

The Kaddish prayer (including the Full Kaddish, Hatzi (Half) Kad-dish, and Mourner's Kaddish) all serve as dividers, boundary markers within the service. The Hebrew word *kaddish* קדש has many meanings, one of them being to divide or to make distinct. The Kaddish signals to us that a transition is about to occur: One part of the service is ending and another part is beginning.

As I reflect upon this literary device, I wish I had some Kaddish markers in my own life that would serve as my "Beware—transition time occurring." How helpful would it have been to have received an alert that my sweet toddler was moving into his more rambunctious "NO!" phase or to have been alerted that mood swings due to hormonal changes were on their way. Unfortunately, our lives are not demarcated that clearly. Fortunately, life happens more organically. In reality, most changes occur gradually, innocuously, transpiring gently over time; nonetheless, there is still a sense of loss as we look back. Where has the time gone? How did my babies turn into their own grown selves? Yes, for me, the changes have been hard and challenging, and yet there remains a sweetness accompanied by a large dose of gratitude associated with the boundaries that demarcate my children's lives.

Words, visions, and items take on new meaning. I know that I won't ever look at shaving cream or fairies in quite the same way. Each now has its own story and memory. We go through parenthood without warnings of transitions; however, our children will naturally draw boundaries when they need their space to grow into the people they are meant to become. The bittersweet challenge of being a parent means that we strive to honor their requests for independence and freedom while simultaneously affixing them to our memories.

It is in supporting our children's desire for boundaries that we allow them the wings that they need to fly into fully actualized human beings. By allowing them the freedom to create the boundaries they need to define themselves, and by encouraging them to figure out their likes and dislikes, their spark of God reveals itself to the world. In essence, these boundary moments become the portals through which God becomes great and magnified. When our children develop their passions, their loves, and their desires, they happily and joyfully add to the world.

And so, alas, there will be no more fairies in my daughter's room. Seeing the happiness in her eyes as a fresh coat of paint updates her walls, her joy dilutes my nostalgia for the fairies.

ב

Y'hay sh'may rahbah m'vahrach
l'ahlahm oo–l'ahlmay ahlmahyah.

Let God's great name be blessed forever and ever.

I am sitting with my son in a small Spanish beach town. The sun is shining, a few scattered clouds are in the sky, pebbles create the "sand" on the beach. We sit, watching our friends and other family members skip rocks into the sea. The two of us sit in silence, listening to the birds and the people surrounding us. Then my son turns to me and says out of the blue, "I am so grateful. I am so grateful to God for everything. I mean, most people don't realize how lucky they are. We all just take so much for granted. I am so grateful that I can feel the rocks beneath me. I am so grateful that I can feel the warmth of the sun and see the sky and the clouds. I am so grateful that I can see my family and friends having fun, skipping rocks. I am so grateful that I can hear their laughter. I mean, Mom, it doesn't get much better than this."

If I weren't sitting down, I think I would have fallen over! Holy wow—this was not a comment I was expecting to hear from my 13-year-old son. How could I respond to that? Feeling completely inadequate, I mustered up what felt like a cheap response, "What an insightful and thoughtful comment," I told him. "How lucky you are to have such an innate sense of gratitude; it will serve you well. Living in gratitude will bring you much joy in your life." And that was that, the conversation ended as quickly as it had started.

While the conversation has ended, its memory still lingers in my mind. There are days that I glance at my son, out of the corner of my eye, and I am transported back to that magical moment in Tossa de Mar. It is in these moments that I am reminded of the incredible teaching role my children have played in my life. I am grateful for their presence in my life and for the ongoing lessons they reveal for me, even when I am not always ready or willing to receive them.

When we read and speak the words of the Kaddish, we have the unique ability to connect to our own experiences of gratitude and grandeur. This line in the prayer,

Y'hay sh'may rahbah m'vahrach l'ahlahm oo-l'ahlmay ahlmahyah
Let God's great name be blessed forever and ever.

is the congregational response to the prayer leader's initial praise of God. It is as if upon hearing the praising of God, we say, "Right on! We agree with you! God is great!" When we each speak these words, we are vouching that we will be partners in blessing God's name forever and ever.

By joining in this communal chanting, together we profess the greatness of God in our collective consciousness, as well as in our own individual consciousness. At this moment, we are given a gift—a gift of reflection, the ability to reflect back on a time in our own lives when we felt this grandeur and gratitude. Each of us can reflect back on a time when we felt the power of God's goodness and magnificence. It is in these moments where we can stop to notice... pause... reflect... and breathe amid the busyness of our lives. By taking time out and expressing gratitude, we create spaces between the hectic activities of our lives. With the goal of being more mindful, pausing allows us the expansiveness to move into "Kaddish/boundary consciousness."

Each time I think back to that wonderful day on the beach, with my son praising God, God is once again praised. Chronologically, the event ended months ago, but in time-space reality, it is happening right now. Conjuring up the memory brings it back, front and center, to my reality. In actuality, through our thoughts, words, and deeds we have the power to ensure that God's name becomes blessed forever and ever.

ג

Yitbahrahch v-yishtahbahch v-yitpah'ayr
v-yitromahm v-yitnahsay, v-yit'hahdahr
v-yit'ahleh v-yit'hahlahl sh'may d'koodshah

Let the name of the Holy Blessed One
be glorified, exalted, and honored,
though Adonai is beyond all the praises,
songs, and adorations
that we can utter.

"You did such a great job on your test!"

"You were amazing on the field!"

"You rocked out last night at your performance!"

"You are such a great friend!"

"You really hit it out of the ballpark!"

"You handled yourself with such grace under pressure!"

"You were terrific out there on the court!"

One of the greatest challenges for me as a mom is to "tone it down." What do I mean? By nature, I tend to be quite—shall we say—expressive. I want to be supportive and encouraging to my kids as they try new activities and attempt to overcome challenges. While two of my three kids respond well to this kind of lauding, one of them detests it. From an early age, my oldest never took to praise. It was a strange concept for me to grasp, but when I would offer praise, he would actually refuse it, negate it, or ignore it.

Interesting... I thought everyone loved to be praised. I discussed this quandary with my husband, as I sincerely didn't get it. Luckily, my husband and son are cut from the same cloth so he totally got it.

"Please, explain it to me," I begged.

"It's not that he doesn't want or like the praise, the problem is in how you are delivering it. You are too effusive, too excited; it's just too much for him."

"OK," I replied, feeling hurt and rejected. Here I was thinking I was being a great mom by supporting and encouraging him. But apparently my praise was falling on deaf ears, and instead of helping him feel better about himself, I was actually doing the opposite. It seemed that I had crossed a boundary of his that I didn't even know existed. This emotional boundary was one that I wanted to honor even if it was not how I normally communicate.

And so began my trials of how to express praise in a way that he could hear it. First, I began by removing the high level of excitement in my voice. Next, I dropped the tone of my voice and expressed myself as nonchalantly as I possible could. Finally, I limited my sentences to only a few words. It was an arduous process and there were many times when I'd look over to see my husband frantically waving his hand in the air, gesturing to me, to cut it off—"Enough!" his hands would say.

After many years of practice, I now know how to respect my son's emotional boundaries. There are times, of course, that I slip up, as the way he needs me to communicate with him goes against my nature, but I have chosen to change because I want a meaningful relationship with him.

When we read these words in the Kaddish, we indicate to God that we want a relationship with Her as well. We offer praise, adoration, glorification, and more. Eight verbs follow one another in the Kaddish. We are reminded through this profound list that we can deepen our relationship with God by offering praise and appreciation, the same way we can deepen our relationship with those individuals we hold dear.

The origin of the Kaddish is unknown, but the oldest version of this prayer is found in the prayer book of Rav Amram Gaon from the ninth century. Through these words the rabbis illustrated the power of praise as a component of intimacy. While I believe that God and most people can handle the intensity of adoration, there are some people, like my son, who have differing levels of receptivity. As we move toward greater intimacy in our relationships, it is important to note the role of praise and the way in which it is delivered. As I learned the hard way, kids hear and integrate praise differently.

Nonetheless, my greatest lesson in this process has been my intuitive understanding to change the delivery of praise and not to eliminate it completely. Initially, I was hurt and decided to remove all compliments if he didn't want to hear them. Then, I took some deep breaths and decided to act maturely. I realized that it was up to me to figure out how to praise him in a way that didn't overwhelm him. I'm glad I listened.

Ways to Promote Healthy Boundaries

1) Create various places in your home such as a reading nook, a play space, or a meditation area. These spaces can include a simple pillow or blanket on the floor.

2) Communicate often, sharing what kind of boundaries and space each family member needs.

3) Arrange each child's sleeping area with special items that belong solely to him/her.

4) Encourage knocking on doors before entering one another's room.

Boundaries: Questions to Consider

1) How important are boundaries to you as a person? As a parent?

2) What kind of boundaries did you grow up with as a child? How do you think they have influenced the way you see boundaries as an adult?

3) What kind of boundaries would you like to establish for your children?

4) How frequently and what kind of praise do you offer your children?

5) Are you able to stop during your day to create boundaries that include gratitude moments?

Confidence
(Ein Keloheinu)

א

Ein Keloheinu.

None is like our God.

One night as I was tucking my daughter into bed, she told me she couldn't fall asleep. We started talking about miscellaneous things, and then she blurted out, "Sometimes I just hate myself. I'm so stupid. I can't do anything right and I'm really bad at spelling. Sometimes I feel that I don't want to even live anymore." PANIC! What I wanted to do at that moment was shake my daughter and scream, "What, are you crazy?! Do you know how lucky you are?" Thank goodness, my wiser half got control and instead I sat quietly for a few minutes, just holding her. How I just wanted to wave my magic mom wand and make it all go away. The pain of watching your child experience feelings of incompetence—as an eight-year-old, nonetheless—wanting very much to fix it for her, to make her realize all of her strengths and talents.

I quickly realized that I just might have the chance to turn this into a learning opportunity. For as much as I wanted to make it all better, deep down I knew better. I knew that she would have this feeling over and over again in her life; well, maybe not about spelling, but surely about something else—reading, friendships, decision-making, parenting.

And so I held my daughter very tightly and sat with her in silence. I validated her feelings and told her how hard it must be to carry those feelings.

After a few minutes, I asked her if she knew that she was the only one in the world who had her fingerprints. "No," she replied. I continued to tell her that out of the billions upon billions of people in the world, she was the only one with her fingerprints, that no one else in the whole world had her fingerprints. And guess what? It is that way with everyone; everyone has their own set of fingerprints because everyone is unique and can never be replaced by anyone else. By this point she seemed more intrigued than sad, so I continued.

"What do you think God would say if He heard that you wanted to give up because you felt that life was too hard?"

Silence. "I don't know."

"Well, let's suppose that God created you to do something really amazingly special—and we know that you are special because of your fingerprints—and then you felt discouraged so you gave up. You know all of us are created in the image of God, so what would that mean to God if you gave up?"

Again silence.

"I know I'm just your mom and you're going to say that I'm supposed to say these kinds of things, but I'm going to say it anyway. I know that you are going to do great things in this world, even if you're not the greatest speller. You're kind and smart, caring and compassionate, sensitive and beautiful. You are incredibly special, and God and I would both be very sad if you decided to give it up and not do what God sent you down here to do. Look at your fingers the next time you are feeling sad, and think about how special you are, how you and only you have those fingerprints."

Smile... finally a smile. Then a hug and an "I love you, Mom."

Ein Keloheinu, none like our God, comes to teach us that yes, there is none like You, Our God, and there is none like each of us. In the book of Genesis, we read that God created us in God's image; therefore, there is none like *You* and there is none like *you*. There is none like God and there is none like each one of us.

We read in the book of Genesis 1:26, "And God said: 'Let us make *adam* (man) in our image, after our likeness.'" The rabbinic commentators notice something unusual about this sentence and ask the question: to whom was God talking? Why does the text use the third person? Why doesn't it say, "Let me make man in *My* image, after *My* likeness?" While the Midrash imagines God consulting with the angels, there is another interpretation that I prefer: Perhaps God was speaking to the animals. God suggests that a human being is created to be both animal-like and

God-like. In some ways, we are like animals: needing to eat, drink, sleep, and mate. In other ways we are like God: capable of compassion, creativity, morality, and self-consciousness.* How do we recognize and welcome our "animal" tendencies, yet strive to be more God-like? I believe it is the integration of these two that remains our life's work.

Ultimately, this message from Genesis is that there is none like you—human beings—you are unique, different from all other species. I would add that, in turn, each of us as human beings is unique and special. As shared by the Mishnah, "When a human being mints many coins with the same stamp, all come out identical, yet the King of Kings, the Holy One, Blessed be God, minted men in the image of Adam, yet not one of them resembles another." **

So how do we teach our children that they are special and unique, especially when many kids who do "march to the beat of a different drummer" are made fun of and teased? Well, despite my kids telling me, "You're just saying this because you are my mom," I still tell them regularly how special they are. Now, I don't advocate going overboard and praising them for silly things, but I do advocate pointing out their real strengths and talents. If your child is an exceptional artist, be sure to hang up her artwork around your house. If your child rocks as a musician, be sure to have him entertain for your family and friends. If your child's athletic ability leaves you in the dust, be sure to attend games regularly and to display trophies in prominent positions. Point out the specifics of their talents.

In my experience, gross generalizations fall flat. Saying, "You're awesome!" or "Great job!" eventually loses its appeal, especially as your child matures. Another way I try to ensure praise is by creating situations in which I will be *kvelling* ("bragging") about what one of my children did and sharing that with a friend. Strategically, I place myself so that my child can overhear what I am sharing. Yes, I know it is a bit sneaky, but I would have said it anyway, and besides, there is something special about hearing nice things said about you when you are "eavesdropping" on a grown-up conversation.

I haven't heard anything else from my daughter about our conversation,

* Eitz Hayim Chumash p.9
** Mishnah, Sanhedrin 4:5

and over the years she has become a better speller. Who knows what stuck and what was forgotten, what was planted and what will germinate over time? But I do know that I have a super special little girl, who I hope one day grows up to know it, too.

ב

Ein Kadoneinu, Ein K'Malkeinu...

None like our Master, None like our Sovereign...

I will never forget the sick feeling in the pit of my stomach the moment I discovered the graffiti on my 12-year-old's wall. He had written some *very* unkind words about my husband and me underneath a picture. When we removed the frame and saw what he had written, we felt like someone had punched us in the gut. Recognizing that he was on the cusp of turning 13, my husband and I paused, smiled, and discreetly glanced at one other with a knowingness of remembering our own teen years. We did not yell; rather, we turned this graffiti outburst into a lesson in painting his walls to remove his remarks. He needed to take responsibility for his actions.

That seems to be a theme in my house: How can I help my children take ownership of their actions, for good and for bad? I've lost count of various and sundry assignments, lunchboxes, shoes, etc., that have been left at home. Why listen to your parent reminding you to pack up the night before school when you can just leave the item at home? As my kids got older, they each received a "get out of jail free card" once a semester and then, after that, they were on their own. They had to accept whatever consequences came their way.

While I am certainly here to help and guide my kids, I want them to know and believe that they are the masters of their own destinies. It is important for them to be responsible for their actions. One of the running jokes my husband and I have with our kids is that one of our favorite aphorisms is "Accept responsibility." They now anticipate these words even before we utter them. I don't want to come across as an insensitive hard-ass; however, I do believe that part of growing into a healthy adult means being able to take ownership of errors.

We see it all around: the hit-and-run drivers, the inability of politicians to admit they have made a mistake. Reading the paper or checking social media will reveal the challenge of being truthful. I get it, I really do. It's scary for me to admit when I've made a mistake, but honestly, I feel much better after I do take ownership. If we as adults are not comfortable enough to be able to take responsibility, how can we expect our children to learn accountability? What messages are we sending them and how is their confidence affected when we coddle them and allow them to neither speak their truth nor accept consequences for their actions? *Ein Kadoneinu, Ein K'Malkeinu* comes to teach us that in order for our children to have confidence in themselves as human beings, they have to be willing to step up to the plate and be their own Masters, to be their own Sovereigns—even if the repercussions are scary.

I believe that our children gain confidence from knowing that they are in control of their bodies, decisions, and actions. By teaching them helpful ways of expressing emotions, they build self-esteem. Reflecting back on the time when my son was feeling frustrated, punched a hole in his bedroom wall, and then got grounded, I hope he realized that it was not such a great idea after all. However, writing in a journal to channel his energy appropriately, without getting grounded—I hope he saw that as a much better idea. Human beings, like other mammals, learn via cause and effect. While we like to think that we are more evolved than mice or dogs, we get conditioned the same way. If x, then y. If I put a hole in the wall, then I'm going to get punished. If I write in my journal, I will hear positive comments regarding my choice.

Judaism teaches that each of us has two inclinations, a *yetzer ha-tov* and a *yetzer ha-ra,* a good inclination and an evil inclination. Evil in this case doesn't mean the kind of evil we think of in the traditional sense. In fact, the rabbis were sure to outline the importance of the *yetzer hara*: "Were it not for the *yetzer hara* (the evil urge), a man would not build a house, take a wife, beget children, or engage in commerce."[*] So the evil inclination is not pure evil; rather, it is the creative, impulsive energy that motivates us. Nonetheless, this *yetzer ha-ra* needs to be kept in check, needs to be

---

[*]Bereishit Rabbah 9:7

channeled in appropriate ways. When raising very young children, we tend to see more of the *yetzer ha-ra*, be it hitting, pinching, biting, pushing, or teasing. While some may say it is the *yetzer ha-ra* that needs to be tamed (which it very well might be), others may call it a child's will. I believe that as parents it is our job to help our children channel their energies in an appropriate way, enabling our children to function and fit into the world.

As I've come to experience it, our challenge is to figure out how to work with each child's balance between the *yetzer ha-tov* and the *yetzer ha-ra*. Some kids come with an 80-20 split, others a 20-80 split, and yet others have many different permutations. How we help them understand and navigate their individual nature is some of our greatest parenting work. By empowering our children to see themselves as their own Master and Ruler, they will be better able to identify their inclinations, be they good or evil, and then decide how best to proceed. I know this process is arduous and rocky, and yet it has potential to be rewarding. When our kids have a better understanding of themselves, they can exude the confidence they need to succeed in life.

Ways to Help Build Confidence

1) Help your child identify something they love to do.

2) Expose your child to various activities so that they can find out what they excel in.

3) Support your child in what they love to do—even if it's not what you love to do or had imagined your child would love to do.

4) Listen carefully, without distractions. Truly give your child your full attention.

5) Challenge them with new ideas, venues, and games. Let them see how successful they can be; if not the first time, then with practice.

6) Point out their success stories. Sometimes we don't see things until others point them out.

7) Let them try to solve problems on their own.

ג

Ein Ki'Moshee'einu.

None like You, our Savior.

There are many times in our kids' lives when we want to jump in and
save them. I remember the *brit milah*, the circumcision, of my eldest. I
was recovering from a C-section, learning how to nurse, sleep-deprived,
overwhelmed, and emotionally drained. The morning of his *bris* arrived
and my motherly instincts kicked in; I wanted to "save" my child from the
pain he was about to endure. The *mohel* was careful to explain that certain
hormone levels are highest on the 8th day of life, so it doesn't hurt as much
as we think. Blah... blah... blah... While he might have been medically on
point, my Mama Bear nature still wanted to jump in and save him. For
my family, not having a *brit milah* was not an option; yet as a new mother,
it was one of the hardest events to which I have ever had to bear witness.

Trying to make sense of this ceremony, several months later, I wrote
the following in his baby book:

> I was very nervous for the *bris*. I knew we would fulfill
> this mitzvah but it was very hard for me to see you cry
> like you did. I wanted to protect you from the pain but I
> guess it was my first experience of wanting to shelter and
> protect you from something inevitable. I pray that your
> life will be blessed with much health and happiness and
> I want you to know that while your Dad and I might not
> always be able to shelter and protect you from pain, we
> will always be here to shelter you with our love, support
> and guidance.

Perhaps part of the hidden wisdom in the *brit milah* ceremony is for
the parents to recognize their inability to always save their children from
painful situations, be they physical, emotional, mental, or spiritual. At
least that is how I rationalized the moment for me. Having done so, I did
feel a bit better about trying to understand that experience in light of my

inability to be "Mom, the Savior."

As the years have passed, I see even more clearly how hard it is to watch your children get hurt, teased, bullied, or simply ignored. Wiping away tears and trying to coax out stories of what actually happened on the playground can be a daunting feat in the midst of such high emotions. So, I've learned to be patient and supportive, watching them muddle through the typical trials and tribulations of growing up. What I have come to learn is that I can't be the "Savior." Only they can truly "save themselves."

But what does it mean to save yourself? For me, it means to depend on yourself. Yes, you can depend on others, but ultimately, you must be able to rely on YOU! Relying on yourself to navigate through life requires the ability to assess situations from a non-judgmental, non-blaming perspective. It is easy to solve your problems by stating that you're right and everyone else is wrong. As a mom, I strive to provide strategies for my children so they will become introspective, healthy, functioning adults. I believe they will grow to do this by having the ability to look at situations from multiple perspectives, and yet be in a place that allows them to live with compassion, gratitude and authenticity for all those with whom they interact. In order to help my children get to a place of navigating life's challenges, I offer them the following equation:

Compassion + Gratitude + Being True to Yourself =

Saving Yourself

First, start with compassion—compassion for themselves and compassion for others. Looking at the situation from different perspectives and thinking about what others might have been feeling when they acted in a particular manner can be helpful. Maybe their friend didn't really mean what they said, maybe they were in an argument with their parents and they came to school grumpy? Giving others the benefit of the doubt may help to alleviate problems in the first place. There are many variables at play and I work with my kids to explore the various possibilities.

After they have examined the situation from the other's perspective, I encourage them to look at the situation from their own perspective. Finally, I remind them not to beat themselves up too much. If they realize that they indeed were part of the problem, there is always the option to apologize and make amends. One of Judaism's core teachings revolves around the notion of *teshuvah*, repentance or returning. With most situations, there is a chance for a "do-over" and for those times when we can't change the situation, we are always free to change how we respond to it.

Second, I try to teach my kids to live in gratitude, which is not an easy task. When my daughter was asking how she could deal with her jealousy toward a friend, I encouraged her to be grateful. She looked at me quizzically, as if I were crazy. "No, really Mom, that makes no sense." It took a good bit of explaining before she understood what I meant, but when she got it, success! It didn't take away the jealousy, but it did help contextualize it. Refraining from thinking about what others have (there will always be more things to acquire) and what others get to do (there will always be others who do more than you do), and instead focusing on what we do have—bodies that are healthy, legs that walk, eyes that see, ears that hear, a house, food, loving family, pets, a warm bed—fill in your own lists here—is no easy feat for adults, let alone for children. But I contend that training our children early on to live in gratitude will make them happier adults. The research is there to prove it![*]

Finally, I teach my kids: Be True to Yourself. Regardless of what others are doing, saying, feeling, expressing, you must remain true to who you are. When you do, life will flow and you will feel good; even when things don't go your way, you will know that you did what was right for you. As my children get older and move into their teenage years, this becomes even more crucial. It is hard to be True to Yourself when your social group may have few others who are like you. When you are a huge skateboarding fan and no one else even knows who Tony Hawk is—how frustrating! How about being a boy who loves ballet or a girl whose dream is to become a firefighter. As far as we have come, gender stereotypes and social norms often still prevail. Nonetheless, by helping our children be True to Themselves, I believe that they will learn to Save Themselves by listening to their own inner voices. With increased compassion, gratitude, and authenticity, they will have the skills they need to assess a challenging situation and approach it with confidence.

While our children try to figure all of this out, I have come to learn

---

[*] There have been numerous studies that support the connection between gratitude and happiness. One article can be found here: https://www.health.harvard.edu/healthbeat/giving-thanks-can-make-you-happier

that my trying to save my children doesn't promote self-esteem. Rather, being a supportive, loving cheerleader on the sidelines, rooting for growth and success, can help facilitate their process. As much as our kids may not admit liking us by their sides, I believe that by showering them with unconditional love, they will ultimately grow into confident, healthy adults.

Confidence: Questions to Consider

1) What might you do to help your child recognize his uniqueness?

2) How might you be able to help your child realize she is her own "Master"?

3) Do you jump in and try to "save" your children from difficult situations? Examine your response and try to understand where this urge comes from.

4) Examine various areas of your child's life (school, home, friends); how might you be able to give him more independence in those areas?

Ways to Promote Confidence

1) Sign up for a new activity and allow your child enough time to become engaged in order to feel successful.

2) Be sure to point out successes in specific ways, such as, "You did a great job on your art project. I love the way you used a wide palette of color," or "Way to go with your basketball win, your rebounds were outstanding!"

3) Write compliments and place them in plain view—on top of your kid's pillow, taped to the bathroom mirror, or on the kitchen table.

4) Encourage your kids to mentor younger children.

5) Volunteer and engage in community service projects.

6) Go to the local library, check out some books that promote self-esteem, and read them together.

7) Teach kids the skill of "positive self-talk" and practice it with them.

Responsibility

(Aleinu)

א

Aleinu l-shahbay'ahch
lah-ahdon hah-kol,
lah-tayt g'dulah l-yotseir b'reisheet,

[It is upon us to] praise You Source of All.
Your generous work as Creator of All.
You made us one with all of Life.

Our area in South Florida is not known for its extensive tree preserves. Unfortunately, while there are certainly some, my family sees many more homes than fields of trees and nature preserves. On one of our regular drives, my kids and I had observed that over the past several months the tree population in a specific area had been dwindling. A few weeks later, we drove by only to find smoke billowing above what used to be a large plot of land covered with trees. Outrage ensued from my son, "That is terrible, what are they doing there?"

Silence.

"Mom, what are they doing, why are they burning all of those trees?" As I looked off to the side of the road, I saw multiple piles of tree trunks bundled together all over the field.

"They are clearing the field so they can build homes," I replied as calmly as I could, feeling the depths of my own pain and despair.

"Why do they have to do that? There are already enough homes in our area; why do they have to build more and why do they have to kill all of those trees?!"

My twelve-year-old daughter piped up, "It's not all bad. I know the trees are being killed, but think about the new houses that will be built for those who need a house, and think about all of the trees and plants that they will replant around the new houses. They have already destroyed the trees; there is nothing to do about it now."

"You can't ignore the negative," excoriated my son.

"You can focus on the positive," retorted my daughter.

I sat in the front seat and sighed, marveling over this incredible exchange. How did my kids get to be so big with their own ideas, values, and abilities to express themselves so articulately? Trying hard not to take sides, I agreed with both of them. Yes, we must be mindful and respectful toward the environment, and yes, we can choose to focus on the positive when we are presented with a challenging, upsetting situation.

Aleinu—it is incumbent upon us to do both. Three important lessons I learned from this interaction:

• We must show up in responsibility for taking care of Mother Earth.
• We can choose how we view challenging situations.
• We can recognize the complexity of competing truths and conflicting values.

As a parent, I believe that it is part of my job to teach my children these three important lessons, and ironically enough, it is these precise lessons that my children taught me.

> *Aleinu l-shahbay'ahch*
> *lah-ahdon hah-kol,*
> *lah-tayt g'dulah l-yotseir b'reisheet,*

> [It is upon us to] praise You Source of All.
> Your generous work as Creator of All.
> You made us one with all of Life

When our children are taught that they have a responsibility to take care of our planet, when they can find good in a difficult situation, when they are able to articulate their values AND listen to another's point of view, they are praising God and God's creation of the world. Just as I was pleased with the conversation that ensued in my car, I imagine God, as the Ultimate Parent, delighting in Her children's conversations. Discussing, arguing, listening, and working to solve how we are going to make this world a better place for all of God's creations is a form of praise to the Sovereign of all things.

Life is messy, complicated, and nuanced. There are many factors we deal with on a regular basis, and conflicting values often emerge. In one conversation three very big issues were raised, and it is difficult to address all of them— especially right in the moment. It took me a while to sit back, reflect, and process what had happened in a short five-minute conversation. Our lives move at such a fast pace, and it is hard to recognize, comprehend, and ultimately make sense of what we see, hear, and experience.

Aleinu—it is our job to sit back, reflect, and integrate.

As parents we can teach our children these same skills. While content is crucial, I'd like to suggest that process is equally important. Creating the space for our children to feel comfortable talking about BIG issues is crucial, be it the environment, attitude and approach to life's challenges, or competing values. Helping our children articulate their own values and encouraging them to see another's point of view is, I believe, one of the most important jobs as a parent.

Fast forward six months and, ironically, we were passing by this same field when a different permutation of my three children got into a conversation about animal experimentation. My older son was praising the virtues of experimenting on animals and pointing out that through this experimentation many lives have been saved. My daughter was up in arms, negating any benefits because of the death of innocent creatures. And so it went, back and forth, arguing, protesting, each defending his or her own stance.

One day, too soon, they will fly the coop. On that day, I want them to be well-equipped with the skills necessary to behave as responsible, open-hearted adults—adults who not only speak their Truth but also hear the Truth of another.

ב

l-tahkein olahm b-mahlchoot shahdai
To restore creation under Your nurturing rule*

---
*http://opensiddur.org/fixed-prayers/aleinu/aleinu-by-joshua-gutoff/

The final prayer that we recite at the end of a service is called *Aleinu* and it speaks about a time when the world will be in perfect harmony. The kind of world we all dream about, where there is enough for everyone; where love, respect, admiration, and deep unity abound. Translated into English, *Aleinu* means "it is upon us." Each of us is called to help move our world toward the goal of Oneness. "And on that day, God shall be One and God's name shall be One." It is that sense of unity that reminded me of a story my son had shared with me over the course of his high school career.

At the beginning of my son's freshman year, he encountered another new student, Mohammed, in his theater class. During the first week, the two of them found themselves at the same lunch table when the topic of Israel came up. Each of them speaking from their own beliefs: Eitan defending Israel; Mohammed defending the Palestinians while decrying the Israel Defense Forces. After quite a few minutes of heated debate, they walked away from the conversation, and from each other.

As the year progressed, Eitan and Mohammed found each other in close proximity during theater class, club, and performances. They slowly moved toward one another, smiling, speaking a few words, until one day they finally struck up a casual conversation, which led to an actual friendship. In fact, after a school drama trip that Eitan did not attend, Mohammed came home with a gift for Eitan, a book on Jewish humor.

Midway through the year, the two friends now shared favorite Middle Eastern foods such as pita, hummus, and za'atar. They compared notes about their respective cultures, Jewish jokes, and things only Jewish or Muslim parents do. On more than one occasion, Eitan has told me, "We are so much more similar than we are different!"

This understanding on both sides has led to a wonderful friendship. When politics emerge in their history class and the topic of Jewish-Arab relations rears its head, both boys look each other in the eyes, smile, and remain silently respectful toward one another. Many months have passed since that first encounter in the cafeteria, and in the middle of March, Eitan recounted a story of the two of them walking to class when Mohammed said, "You know, it's a shame that Arabs and Jews can't be friends like us."

As he shared this story with me, I literally burst into tears, and like any 15-year-old boy, Eitan exclaimed, "Whoa, Mom, no tears, no tears, please." I simply couldn't help it. The beauty of their encounter completely overwhelmed me. I pray for the day when all people can see each other as human beings, all part of a greater human race. Seeing the humanity and divinity in one another, we will exclaim, "Enough! That is enough! No more wars, no more bloodshed, no more killing."

Aleinu—it is upon us to do the work, to fix our broken world, to restore creation under God's nurturing rule, one relationship at a time.

One of God's many names is *El-Shaddai*. While its origins are unclear, there is a teaching that this name comes from the Akkadian, meaning mountain. Interestingly, the modern Hebrew word for breasts is *shadayim*. The images conjured up by mountains and breasts can be seen as an expression of the female qualities of the Divine. A complementary teaching breaks up the name El-*Shaddai* to El She-Dai, meaning: the God who knows when enough is enough. Just like a breastfeeding mother, whose breasts learn how to regulate themselves according to the baby's needs, so too, is this name for God one in which "enough" is in balance.

Perhaps in addition to understanding "*l-tahkein olahm b-mahlchoot shahdai*" to mean, "to restore creation under Your nurturing rule," it can also point us to a time when the inhabitants of the world will come to say, "*she-dai*—Enough!" We no longer agree to live in a way that is incompatible with seeing the humanity in one another.

Enough! That is enough! No more wars, no more bloodshed, no more killing. We acknowledge that we all come from the same Source, even if we access that Source in a multitude of ways.

May the friendship between these two boys begin to pave our path toward kindness, decency, respect, and love for each other.

Ways to Promote Responsibility

1) Create a job wheel in order to share chores around the house.
2) Teach children to take care of their
personal space, toys, clothes, etc.
3) Have older siblings look after younger
siblings, cousins, or neighbors.
4) When kids are old enough, encourage them to get a job, even
if it is yard work, additional house cleaning, or babysitting.
5) Model responsibility for your children so
they come to understand the importance,
potency, and longevity of responsibility.

Responsibility: Questions to Consider

1) What role does responsibility play in your own life?
2) Is there a difference between being responsible and taking
responsibility for one's actions? If so, what is the difference?
3) How do you encourage being responsible and taking
responsibility for one's actions in your family?
4) In what ways can you support your children
growing into responsible adults?

The Big Picture
(Mourners' Kaddish)

א

Yitgahdahl v-yitkahdash
sh'may rahbah b-ahlmah divrah chir'ootay

Let the glory of God be extolled.
Let God's great name be hallowed, in the
world whose creation Adonai willed.

One night in 2011 as we were preparing for a bat mitzvah party, I noticed that my son's belt was torn. My husband came to the rescue and lent him one of his, but it was not any regular belt; it was special, having belonged to his father, who had passed away in 1995. My son, who is named after this grandfather, was aware of the significance of this borrowed offering.

We had a wonderful time at the event, but upon arriving home, my husband discovered that the belt had been left at the party. It was 1:00 a.m. and nothing was to be done about it at that late hour, as the club was closed and everyone was exhausted. I could sense my husband's anger and disappointment as he, himself, had held onto this belt for over 20 years and now, in one night, it had been lost. When his father died, my husband took very few of his father's personal items; one of them was this black leather belt.

As my son got into bed and realized that he had indeed lost this very special heirloom, he began to cry. It wasn't a regular cry, it was more of a wail. We let him cry for about five minutes, and as his sobs got louder and louder, I could hear him feeling the depth of what he had left.

I waited outside his room and watched my husband enter. As I listened in, I heard my husband talk about what had happened. In an unbelievably calm tone, my husband began to speak to him about how and why he had lost the belt. As he spoke I could still hear my son crying. To be honest, I don't recall hearing him cry like that since he was a little boy. Gently, my husband asked him to stop crying in order for him to hear what he wanted to share about his father.

He began, "When my father died, he wanted to be cremated so that none of us would be attached to going to a place to visit him. He wanted us to remember him in our hearts at all times. He didn't want to be remembered by his things, but rather by the kind of person he was. My father was a man who did not have many things that he treasured. Sure, he loved things, but he was not attached to them. I am certain that he would not have wanted to be remembered by a belt. Yes, it was nice to have one of his belts as a tangible reminder, but not so that he could be remembered. What is more important is that you learn from tonight's experience. When you have something of value that belongs to you or to someone else, you have to be mindful of it. You have to make sure you pay close attention at all times to its whereabouts. That's what I hope you've learned. I'm not upset with you; I still love you very much."

He hugged him and kissed him and tucked him in bed. After listening to this most incredible encounter, I wiped my tears away and walked to my room to get myself ready for bed. Having witnessed this monologue was both humbling and inspiring. I imagine that part of my husband really wanted to scream, "Are you kidding me, what is wrong with you? How could you be so irresponsible? You are always losing things and now this—an item that is irreplaceable?!" But instead, he showed love and compassion and de-escalated what could have been a major blowup.

The irony of this occurrence transpiring on May 5, the exact date on which my father-in-law had passed away, was not lost on me. While I am unsure of the spiritual significance, I do believe there is much to be learned about how we remember those we love most; about how we are attached to the material items that our loved ones touched and wore; and most importantly, about how we love the ones who are still alive, next to us, crying when they are hurt and torn to their core.

Kudos to my amazing husband who handled himself with incredible patience and love. When we spoke later that night, I commended him on a job well done and he responded by sharing, "What was I supposed to do? It was more important that I not damage his psyche. It was only a belt and his psychological well-being certainly needed to take priority."

Yes, sometimes, indeed, we get to witness parenting successes and I knew I had witnessed one on that fateful night. As parents, we try our best, hoping that what we are teaching and modeling will help put our children on the path toward *menschlichkeit* (becoming honorable, upstanding, compassionate citizens). Unfortunately, one of the drawbacks is that our investment is long term. The majority of our efforts that go into child-rearing are most often not seen... and then there are those moments of grace when you get the privilege of seeing a parenting success.

So how is it that through our parenting we have the opportunity to make God's name great and holy? We read in the book of Genesis that God created people in God's own image. How so? By breathing into the nostrils of Adam. Through that process, we as humans became infused with God's breath and God's life-force. Each time we act in a way that is kind and compassionate, we are allowing that God-part in each of us to shine forth and become magnified.

It is easy to get lost in the overwhelming, ever-flowing, all-surrounding details of life. Just when I think I can check something off my to-do list, three more things appear in its place. No matter how hard I try to organize, there always seems to be things that I forget. The running joke in my family is that despite the number of times a week I may be at the grocery store, I will inevitably have forgotten something. And so it goes...

Parenting and life in general just seem to be that way. I have worked hard to get myself to a place of acceptance, acknowledging that sometimes I won't get it right, won't remember it all, and won't be completely organized. Through all of these misgivings, I continue to work on forgiving myself. By forgiving myself, I am thrust into the big picture of Things That Really Matter And Make A Difference In Life. Yet, it remains challenging for me to stay focused on the big picture when all the details constantly pull me down. I try to remind myself that I'm doing the best I can. I love my kids; I'm there for them even if I can't ever seem to have my pantry stocked, even when I don't remember to buy leotards for gymnastics camp or tennis shoes for tennis camp, or a dress belt for a bat mitzvah. I know there are plenty of things I just won't accomplish.

Then there are those moments when I get to see the Big Picture playing itself out right in front of me. Showing love and compassion in the midst of anger and disappointment. Providing support and guidance despite the inability to master the details. It is a challenge for me, for all of us, but the Mourner's Kaddish is here to remind us of the Big Picture: that through our actions and our deeds, we have the power to make God's name great and holy in all that we do and perhaps even, in all that we don't.

ב

Yitbahrahch v-yishtahbahch v-yitpah'ayr v-yitromahm v-yitnahsay, v-yit'hahdahr v-yit'ahleh v-yit'hahlahl sh'may d'koodshah

Glorified and celebrated, lauded and worshipped, acclaimed and honored, extolled and exalted may the Holy One be...praised beyond all song and psalm.

The other night my daughter came into my room gasping, "I need a breathing treatment." I jumped out of bed, followed her to her room, glanced at the kitchen clock, which read 4:06 a.m., turned on her light, and quickly assembled her nebulizer. Within 20 seconds I had the inhaler piece in her mouth. No matter how many times I have done this (unfortunately probably hundreds), I am always panicked that my child will somehow, God forbid, stop breathing. After a few puffs, she relaxed and subsequently, I relaxed. For a few moments I sat on her bed, then stood up to turn off her lights.

Suddenly, I noticed a crumpled tissue on the floor. I picked it up and saw writing on it: "A person I create, Every person has a meaning."

"What is this?" I inquired.

"Oh, that is a message from God," my daughter replied nonchalantly.

"Really. Ok, well I want to hear more about it, but it's 4:00 a.m. now, so let's talk in the morning."

"Okay. Love you, Mom."

"Love you too, Bat-Ella."

The next morning I asked Bat-Ella what was on that crumpled tissue. She started to explain to me, "Mom, I had a conversation with God. Well, I'm not sure if it was God or myself talking to myself, but I asked God why He created Hitler if He knew that Hitler would be so mean and do so many bad things. And God answered me and I wanted to remember what He said, so I wrote it down."

"Do you understand what it means?"

"No."

"Well the next time you talk to God, remind Him that you are nine and that He might want to answer a little less cryptically," I suggested with a smile.

I am constantly amazed at my daughter's ability to converse with God. This isn't the first time she's told me that she talks to the Divine, but it is the first time she's written the response down. I took the tissue and tucked it away in her keepsake book.

As the day went on, I kept replaying that conversation in my mind. In those few moments my nine-year-old daughter taught me so much. She modeled for me the importance of talking to God, questioning God, and recording what you hear. She also showed me her self-sufficiency and her self-reliance. Although as her mom I always want to be with her, protecting her from harm and pain, I know that's unrealistic. There will be times when I won't be there to answer a question for her, or to wipe her tears, or to wave my magic wand and make it all better, but she provided me with a glimpse of her ability to tap into her Self, to reach inward, upward, and outward to God. She taught me that she intuitively knows that ultimately she is never alone.

Without her even knowing it, she was living out the words of the Kaddish. While some may say that glorifying, celebrating, lauding, worshipping, acclaiming, honoring, extolling, and exalting God must take place in a synagogue, or through a specific prayer or ritual, I believe that any of these acts toward God can happen at any time, in any place. We can glorify God by speaking kindly to our children. We can celebrate God by acknowledging a beautiful sunset. We can worship, acclaim, and honor God when we help with a beach cleanup. We can extol and exalt God when we refrain from speaking badly about others. There are myriad ways to praise God.

For me, on that night, my daughter glorified, celebrated, lauded, worshipped, acclaimed, honored, extolled, and exalted God—by speaking to, connecting with, and reaching out to the Holy One of Blessing. Knowing that she is able to connect to something so much bigger and grander than anything she might even imagine, makes me proud of her ability to tap into the Big Picture—The Big Picture of the Mysterious Nature and Existence of God.

My experience in general has been that kids are much more comfortable talking about and believing in God than adults are. As grownups, we have had more time to move further away from what were born knowing. We have had years of intellectual input and scientific repudiation of the existence of God. Most of us don't feel comfortable or well versed enough in language to begin to describe any spiritual experiences we may have had over the course of our lives. Kids are not as jaded; they are more open to the possibility of talking about God and Her place in our world.

As a parent, it is crucial for me to have my kids exposed to the possibility of God's existence. If the name God feels uncomfortable for them, they can call it Universal Life Force, Energy, Mystery, Something Other and Beyond. I don't care what they call it, as long as they acknowledge it. As much as we try, there are some things in this world that are unexplainable, incomprehensible, and unimaginable. For me, that is where God comes in. There is a BIG PICTURE out there and, if we are lucky, in our lifetime, we receive a glimpse of this giant puzzle.

Life is so much bigger than we imagine. One of my favorite Hasidic teachings comes from Reb Simcha Bunim of Peshischa, who taught that each of us should carry two pieces of paper, one in each of our pockets. The paper in one pocket reads, "I am nothing but dust and ashes" and in the other, "For me, the entire world was created." Living with this balance allows us to acknowledge the Big Picture, by reminding us that while our problems may seem monumental, we are really nothing but dust and ashes. And yet, simultaneously, each of us is so special that the entire world was created just for us. This is what I want my kids to know—each of them has a gift so special that only they can bring it to the world, and yet, they are only dust and ashes. So when the going gets tough... place your troubles into a bigger context, into the Big Picture of what is really happening.

Through our singing of God's praises, speaking our deepest truths and fears, and connecting to the Divine, we are catapulted into the realm of the Unknown, into the Big Picture. I learned all of this as I reflected back on my daughter's crumpled tissue, which actually makes me want to go grab my own.

ג

Y'hay sh'lahmah rahbah min sh'mahyah v-chahyeem
Aleinu v-ahl kol yisrah'ayl v-imroo Ahmein.

May peace abundant descend from heaven,
with life for us and for all Israel, and let us say: Amen.

I can't understand it. Every day when I am on the way to pick my daughter up from school, I inevitably get a call from her asking to have a playdate. Of course, this is after I had reminded her daily that we don't have playdates during the week. By the time she gets home, it's close to four, then snack, some chill-out time, homework, after-school activities, dinner, and a bit more relaxing time, shower, then bedtime. She knows the routine and yet, it never fails, she still calls. When my phone rings at 3:14 p.m. (pick-up is at 3:15 pm), I know who it is and how the conversation will unfold. I now answer with "Hi, Bat-Ella." I must admit there are some days (when I know she has no homework and no after school activities) that I will allow a playdate, so I guess she's hoping for one of those days when she calls. I can't blame her for trying.

She is by far my most social child. On weekends when I don't have plans arranged, she goes a bit bonkers. She loves playing with friends and being surrounded by people. I encourage her to take some quiet time, to go to her room to read, or color, or listen to music, and she begrudgingly acquiesces. But if truth be told, she thrives in the company of other people.

For her, there is something life-giving that feeds her essence when she is in the presence of others. Her smile is glowing, her laugh contagious, her joy infectious. Having recently read several articles attesting to the importance of community, the findings indicate that individuals who have a group of friends or a community to whom they are attached, live longer. Those who are socially isolated die earlier. It is clear that being with other human beings nourishes our spirits, enriches our lives, and apparently lengthens our days. I guess my daughter is on to something. Perhaps I need to reconsider my no-after-school-playdate rule.

This notion of being part of a community permeates Judaism, especially during a prayer service. While some prayers can be recited solo, the really important ones can only be recited in the presence of a *minyan*, a prayer quorum of ten individuals over the age of 13. The rabbis who mandated these rules must have also known the value of community. The Mourner's Kaddish is one of those prayers that cannot be recited alone; a *minyan* is required. Being with others, especially after the death of a loved one, is crucial and I believe, ultimately, healing.

Fortunately, I have not yet had to recite the Mourner's Kaddish for any immediate relatives, but I have heard from several friends who have recited Kaddish over the course of many months that there is something incredibly comforting and powerful about reciting these words, even when you don't understand them. Perhaps there is something in the alliteration or the cadence that brings comfort. Something in the recitation of these words that helps an individual feel less alone. Whether it is in the actual words themselves or the power of being held by a community of people who pray with you, a space is created in which grief may reside.

What is most interesting about the Mourner's Kaddish is that it makes no reference to death or dying. Rather, the Kaddish is a public sanctification of God's great Name. The prayer begins with the words, "*Yitgahdahl v-yitkahdash,*" which were inspired by the prophet Ezekiel in the book of Ezekiel 38:23.* He imagines a time when God will become recognized and great in the eyes of other nations.

So why might this prayer have been chosen to be recited by a mourner if there is no reference to the deceased? I think there are two reasons. First, Kaddish speaks to the power of community. Human beings are not made to be alone, especially after the loss of a loved one. Second, Kaddish

---

*Thus will I magnify Myself, and sanctify Myself, and I will make Myself known in the eyes of many nations; and they shall know that I am Adonai.

gently reminds us that despite our own sorrow, we are part of something much larger than ourselves. Through the recitation of these words, we acknowledge the Big Picture and the hope that healing will eventually unfold. The cadence and rhythmic nature of the Kaddish may gradually propel us back into life, as we emerge from our mourning.

The line,

Y'hay sh'lahmah rahbah min sh'mahyah v-chahyeem Aleinu v-ahl kol yisrah'ayl v-imroo Ahmein

May peace abundant descend from heaven,
with life for us and for all Israel, and let us say: Amen.

is recited by the entire congregation. With these words, we remind the mourner that as a community we support them, we pray for them, and we pray for abundant peace and goodness. At a time when, for many, the natural response toward the death of a loved one is to turn inward, we are instructed to recite Kaddish daily with a *minyan*, a group of others who are there to remind us of the importance of being in community. Knowing that we are loved and cared for helps us move forward one small step at a time. Perhaps it is this human connection that will bring healing, solace, and strength to those who mourn.

I think back to my daughter's social nature. She intuitively knew that in the midst of her challenges, and her trials and tribulations of growing up, ultimately it is in the strength garnered from being part of a community that will ensure a less tumultuous, more joyful journey for all of us.

Big Picture: Questions to Consider

1) Reflect back on a time where you saw your own parenting miracle. How did you feel experiencing it?

2) How can we strive to examine our child's needs with love and compassion in the midst of our own desire to simply scream?

3) In what ways can you glorify, celebrate, laud, worship, acclaim, honor, extol, or exalt the Holy One?

4) Have you ever felt alone and yet simultaneously supported by a community?

5) What is your social life like? Do you have a strong support network? If not, how might you try to build one?

6) Do you believe that there is a Big Picture for your life? For your family's life?

7) How might you surrender to see pieces of the Big Picture?

Ways to Help See the Big Picture

1) Create a sign that reads "Don't sweat the small stuff" and hang it in a prominent place in your home.

2) Learn several breathing techniques.

3) Practice yoga.

4) Try to see the larger issue and not the smaller issue that is obscuring the Big Picture.

5) Connect to family and friends.

6) Gain perspective with the help of a strong social support network.

God

(Adon Olam)

א

Ahdon Olam ahsher mahlach
bi'teyrem kol yi'tzeer neevrah...
v'hu hahyah v'hu hoveh,
v'hu yi'heeyeh bi'teefahrah...
bi'lee reysheet, bi'lee tahchleet

You were cosmic Lord, ruling*
before there even was a world...
You were, You are, eternally
resplendent to infinity...
Beginningless and without end.

The conversation moves quickly from the Big Bang to the time-space continuum, and I know that I am in over my head. While I am interested in learning about the origins of the Universe, my knowledge base is limited. While Unified Field Theory and the Butterfly Effect are merely hypotheses, my intuition tells me that they are true.** Nonetheless, I know that in the world of science, intuition doesn't cut it. I need facts, proof, and hardcore research to support my hunches. All of this drives my rational, scientific teenager crazy. My nearly 17-year-old son doesn't miss an opportunity to challenge me on my "gut" beliefs. Raised with a strong Jewish background, he now walks around professing his

---

*This originally appears as "You were cosmic Lord, Yah Malach," according to Reb Zalman z"l. We changed the wording to make it more understandable to English speakers.
**Both of these hypotheses contend that all living sentient beings are interconnected and what happens to one of us, happens to all of us. In fact, new research is coming out from astrobiologists and astrochemists that connects human beings' origin to the cosmos. See *The Stardust Revolution* by Jacob Berkowitz to learn more.

disbelief in God and his resentment toward his "indoctrination." Why did we send him to a Jewish school where he would be taught "lies"? Why do I believe in something that has no proof? I received challenges daily, and I responded for a while, really trying to listen thoughtfully. However, I soon realized that our conversations were not dialectical; rather, he wanted to prove his point, regardless of what I had to say. After many months, I finally stopped taking the bait and just listened without responding much.

Although I try to stay quiet, my buttons are often pushed and I struggle to remain silent. A recent conversation left me exasperated once again. It is not just that I disagree with his views, but rather that he tries to change my beliefs through logic and reason. Time and time again, he attempts to chip away at religion; what is most bothersome is his intolerance for another's (mine, in this case) point of view. It was precisely this attitude that I could no longer allow to grow, so I gave him an analogy which I hoped he could contemplate.

From the depths of my months of silence, I was able to share the following: "I'd like to present an analogy to you that I'm hoping will help you to understand that there are various perspectives on this topic. Imagine a prism. Now I want you to shine a colored light on it. While I don't know how the physics of it works, I imagine that if you shine a red light on the prism, it will be reflected and you will see the red reflected; if you take yellow, I surmise that you will see a yellow reflection. Don't ask me if this is 100% accurate, but that's my unscientific guess. Now pretend that Life is your prism and that what you shine on it, is what is reflected. You happen to have a specific scientific perspective, so when you shine science on Life, that is what you will see. Others shine a musical light or a philosophical light, or a theological light—and, depending on what you shine (your perspective), that is what you will see reflected in the prism. You and I have very different perspectives and neither is right nor wrong; it just IS."

I'm not sure what made me say what came out my mouth next, but I continued, "While we see and experience the world differently, I want you to know that I don't need or want you to believe what I believe. I want you to figure out what you believe, AND—despite our theological schism—I love you very much and will always love you, even if you don't believe in God."

For a split second, I saw tears well up in his eyes... and then they were gone.

For a split second, I saw the little boy hidden deep inside my 17-year-old... and then he was gone.

And then I got it. This conversation was not about science or religion; it was not about varying perspectives, it was about unconditional love and presence. It was about knowing that even if he pushed the boundaries and my buttons, I would still love him.

One of God's names, Y-H-V-H, is associated with this kind of love—an unconditional, ever-present love. In the story of the creation of the world, there are two conflicting verses that the Midrash works to reconcile. In Genesis 1:1, we read that *Elohim* created the world. This name for God is representative of judgment. In Genesis 2:4, we read that Y-H-V-H *Elohim* made the heavens and the earth. Why is God called two different names in this similar creation story? The Midrash comes to teach the following:

This may be compared to a king who had some empty glasses. The king wondered: "If I pour hot water into them, they will burst; if, however, I pour cold water, they will contract [and shatter]." What then did the king do? He poured in a mixture of hot and cold water so the glasses would remain whole. So, said the Holy One: "If I create the world on the basis of mercy alone, its sins will be oppressive; on the basis of judgment alone, how would the world be able to exist? I will create it with justice and mercy together and then, maybe, it will be able to stand!" That is why the Name Y-H-V-H is added to the Name *Elohim.*[*]

I've come to understand that parenting requires this same balance—a balance between judgment (*Elohim*) and mercy (Y-H-V-H). On the High Holidays when we beseech God for mercy, understanding, and love, we repeat again and again,

"Y-H-V-H, Y-H-V-H (pronounced *Ahdonay, Ahdonay*), *El Rachum vi'chanun, erech ahpahyeem vi'rav chesed vi'emet.*[**] It is this kindness that reaches to a thousand generations, this love with which the world was

---

[*]Midrash Rabbah on Genesis 12:15.
[**]Exodus 34:6-7, referred to as the Thirteen Attributes of Mercy. "The Lord, the Lord, compassionate and gracious God, slow to anger, abounding in loving-kindness and truth, extending loving kindness to a thousand generations." (translation from the Koren Yom Kippur Machzor, 134.)

created. A love that was built into very existence itself by a God who understood that love is a crucial fabric woven in the tapestry of the world. Love that will exist throughout all time and space. For many years, I have struggled to find a place of peace with my own desire to prove God's existence. Thousands of pages read, hundreds of questions asked, and many sleepless nights, all with the desired goal to figure out the meaning of existence. But alas, after extensive searching, I have not found the answer I sought. What I did find was hope and faith. Along the way, I discovered Jewish sources that spoke to God's "Is-ness": God is, was, and will be, no beginning and no end. It is precisely this name for God, Y-H-V-H, associated with the quality of love, mercy, and compassion, that also is linked to the notion of eternity.

Jewish tradition teaches that the name Y-H-V-H is unpronounceable. If we try to sound it out letter by letter, we hear the sound of a breath, the breath that holds a sense of past, present, and future. In Hebrew the verb for "to be" is based on these same four letters:

H-Y-H   = was
H-V-H   = am/is
Y-H-Y-H   = will be

By configuring these letters into various permutations, the eternality of God Y-H-V-H becomes embedded in this name: God is, was, and will be. Implanted in this Y-H-V-H name resides a sense of love and oneness. According to the Kabbalists, the numerical number associated with Y-H-V-H is 26. The number associated with love (*ahavah*) is 13 and the number associated with the word "one" (*echad*) is also 13. Therefore, we can say that

Y-H-V-H = love + oneness (is/was/will be simultaneously).*

I'm not sure if my words sank into my son's brain, but I'm pretty confident that they sank into his heart; for despite our different beliefs about God and the nature of Their existence, I know that love is the ultimate redemptive power. For me, that power is nestled deep within

---

*The process of assigning numerical values to Hebrew letters is called gematria. Each letter of the alphabet is assigned a value, beginning with the first letter, aleph, which is one.

God's Y-H-V-H name, hidden in the creation of the universe. And while my son wants nothing to do with any kind of God, I hope that he comes to know that the power of love is hidden and expressed deep within his mother's heart, as well as his own.

ב

Bi'lee raysheet, b'lee tachleet, v'loh hah'oz vi'hameezra
Vi'Hoo Eylee, vi'chai go'halee vi'tzur chevlee bi'eyt tzarha.

Beginningless and without end
You keep all one by plan and strength.
You are my God, Redeemer.
Life Protecting me in war, in strife.

I had been sufficiently warned, many times, by many different people, and yet, I still didn't believe that it would happen to me. "Impossible," I thought. "It would be so out of character for her. She is so sweet and we are so connected; it happens to others, but I can't believe that it will happen to us."

And then it did.

Last week was a really hard week with my 13-year-old daughter. She was moody and cranky. She went straight into her room after school, closed the door, got on her computer to talk with her friends, begrudgingly sat with us for dinner, and then went straight back into her room. And when she was with us, she didn't utter a word or crack a smile.

"Who is this girl?" I wondered. "Who absconded with my sweet, caring, talkative, sensitive child?" I was literally in shock, even though I had been warned many times by many different people.

The days passed by ever so slowly. With each rising sun, I hoped that my loving daughter would come back to herself, to the little girl who couldn't get close enough to me. The little girl who would hold my hand and snuggle and tell me that she sometimes wished that she could crawl back inside my tummy. My sweet child who listened intently and followed directions precisely; my girl who told me the exhaustive details of her day, sometimes to the point where I would suggest that maybe it was "TMI" (too much information), wondering how much a daughter should share with a mother.

It wasn't just that she had changed overnight—literally—it was also that I knew something was wrong and she wasn't talking about it. While she seemed to glare at my husband and me, we would hear her through her bedroom door, laughing away and chatting freely with her friends. Completely bewildered, my husband and I wondered together what was going on, and then we strategized how to deal with our newly emerged teenager daughter. Each night as I crawled into bed, I secretly hoped that the daughter I had known for 13 years would return the next day.

The days passed without any luck. When Saturday arrived, I thought things might be different without the stresses of school. Maybe she was just having a hard time getting back into the swing of things after an amazing summer? Maybe she was stressed by all of the homework?

I got dressed for synagogue and was preparing to leave with my son and my daughter. I was wearing a white top and a navy skirt, and my daughter was wearing an all-navy dress. Noticing how we were dressed differently, my son came over and whispered, "Even in her dress, she is contrasting you." I smiled and realized that clearly Bat-Ella's behavior toward me was not in my imagination. Feeling both validated and sad, we got in the car and drove to synagogue. Each week, my daughter has sat next to me and I was, once again, hoping for some reconciliation. Maybe she would revert to her old patterns, but alas, she took the aisle seat, making sure to put my son in between us. Even when my son got up, she refused to sit next to me, preferring the space.

Then, in the middle of services, it hit me and I couldn't hold back my tears. I felt it, the pain of letting go, and the hurt that comes deep from the womb, and the sadness settling in my gut. Then a new emotion arose, one with which I was not familiar, the burning desire to contract, *l'tzamtzem*. It was an odd feeling at first, but I knew it was what my daughter both wanted and needed so desperately. She needed me to perform *tzimtzum*, the act of contracting back into myself to make room for her to emerge. In that moment I realized that her being so connected to me did not allow her the space—literally—to grow into who she needed to be. And the tears kept flowing… this painful realization filled with love and grace. The ultimate sacrifice made by a parent, to pull back and retract into oneself as a way to allow another to emerge into their fullness.

I began to imagine that this is how God must feel. The mystics talk about God as being Infinite, Boundless, Beginningless and Endless. They teach that in order to make room for the world to come into being, God contracted into Godself through a process called *tzimtzum* (Hebrew for contraction). In the beginning all was God; there was no room for anything else. Only when God contracted to make space for the world, could the world come into being. How beautiful and painful a process! The art of self-abnegating in order to see what emerges. What amazing trust and faith is needed for the unfolding of this process.

These words in *Adon Olam* speak this truth:

Bi'lee raysheet, b'lee tachleet,
v'loh hah'oz vi'hameezra.
Vi'Hoo Eylee, vi'chai go'halee
vi'tzur chevlee bi'eyt tzarha.

Beginningless and without end
You keep all one by plan and strength.
You are my God, Redeemer.
Life Protecting me in war, in strife.

God as Everything; Everything as God. Even within Infinity, God managed to constrict a bit, to create space for us. I wonder if God's willingness and desire to create an openness for humanity was also linked with a desire for us to connect to that Infinite Source. Did God desire to be a refuge for us? Were our hearts and our souls sought, as space was cleared for our existence? Wearing my biased, human-centric parent glasses, I'd scream a loud "YES!" Of course that was God's desire, just as it is my desire. Of course I'm willing to give my daughter her space **and** I have a deep desire to connect with her. In reality, I don't pretend to know God's desires, but I do know mine.

I believe that my daughter has everything within her that she needs to grow and succeed, and as painful as it feels for me, I also know that she cannot do it as fully with me constantly present. She needs her space to grow, and that symbolic seat that was left open between us during Shabbat services was actually more than just a symbol. It was a real reminder to me that I must contract, I must perform *tzimtzum,* so that my daughter can have the room to grow into who she is meant to become.

During this painful process, I will turn to God as my redeemer and refuge and hope to find solace and comfort with someone who's "been there, done that." I ask for love and compassion, patience, and freedom from self-judgment—all of which I know I will need along the way. Most poignantly, I pray for the power of memory to remind me of that sweet, delicious little girl that still lives inside this evolving, maturing young woman.

Ways to Connect to God

1) Read books that present various perspectives about God. Having conversations with our children is easier if we have a sense of what our own beliefs are (even if they may change over time).

For Adults:
Finding God, Rifat Sonsino and Daniel B. Syme
God is a Verb, David Cooper
Sacred Fragments, Neil Gillman

For Children:
The Old Turtle, Douglas Wood
God's Paintbrush, Rabbi Sandy Eisenberg Sasso
What Does God Look Like, Lawrence and Karen Kushner

2) Don't be afraid to discuss God and don't be afraid to acknowledge that you don't have an answer.
3) Explore the natural world.
4) Perform *gemilut hasadim*—acts of loving-kindness.
5) Learn to meditate—both adults and kids alike!
6) Find a spiritual home for your family and a spiritual advisor with whom you will feel comfortable.

God: Questions to Consider

1) How do you understand/imagine God?
2) Where do you see God in the world?
3) Have you ever had an experience that you would call God? If so, can you describe it? Discuss as a family.
4) Why do you think it is hard to have conversations about God?
5) What do you think God desires from us?

Epilogue

This book has been 10 years in the making. Ten years filled with struggle, pride, laughter, tears, and love—lots and lots of love. First, I'd like to thank my children for agreeing to allow me to share their stories. And in case you might be wondering, yes, I did receive their permission to go public. I have said on numerous occasions that my children have been my greatest teachers—truly. I'm not sure if they realize how much they have molded and shaped me into the mom and the person that I am today. B.K. (Before Kids) I was not what I would consider a patient person. In fact, I'd call myself a bit impetuous, and to be honest, a bit rigid and okay—I'll admit it—somewhat of a control freak; A.K. (After Kids), not so much.

I remember a defining mommy moment when my boys were about four and two. They were on one side of the house and I had run to the other side to grab a sippy cup. As I opened up the pantry to pull one out, I noticed that the bottom I had grabbed did not have its matching top. B.K., I would have spent some time searching to find its proper match because you know, in my world, things needed to match. I remember standing there for several seconds asking myself, "What should I do—do I just grab what's available or spend a few moments looking for the bottom's missing mate?" Yes, to some, I know this question might sound ludicrous, but it's a true story. In that moment I answered myself, "Screw it, does it really matter?" I ran the mismatched cup to my son, who was now crying. It was a defining moment. I realized then that life is messy and imperfect, that things don't always match, and that it's okay. It is all really okay.

As my kids grew, I had many more sippy cup moments, much more serious and important. Like the times I was called to the principal's office, or the time one of my son's teachers, in a fit of rage toward him, slammed his computer down and cracked the screen. The time when one of my children raised their hand in fury to hit me and the times I spent in doctors' offices to deal with broken bones and medical testing to ensure they were healthy. The millions of events that have occurred over nearly two decades have helped me become more patient, less rigid, more understanding, and more loving. I am forever grateful to my children for being my teachers, for mirroring back to me the parts of myself that I'm not so proud of—and the parts in which I do take pride.

I want to take full responsibility for the retelling of these stories in this book. While my children might not have experienced these events similarly, I want them to know that they have been filtered and written through my lens and my perspective. I pray that if and when they become parents, they will be blessed to learn from their children, to see parenting as a spiritual discipline, as a possibility and gift for personal growth. In re-reading and editing this book, I was struck by how much I had changed in my thoughts and approach. I am not the same person—or the same parent—I was 10 years ago. The chapters that I had originally written years ago needed to be rewritten from a kinder, gentler—dare I say wiser—place. My initial recountings had way too many "shoulds" and "oughts"; in the revised version, most, if not all, of them were removed. I've learned that in parenting, there are no absolutes and using "should" and "ought" is a recipe for disaster. Expectations that are created are often not met, desires that surface are often not fulfilled. And everyone suffers—parents and children. I've learned that children are born with their own personalities, interests, and purposes. How my children have grown and the interests they've pursued are shocking at times and not necessarily what my husband and I would have preferred. Nonetheless, I have come to understand my role of parent to be that of a dependable, nurturing guide. And, in reality, I know that my kids are going to do what they want, how they want to do it. I have learned to accept this reality with grace and humility in order to preserve our relationship.

I have often compared my relationship with my kids to a bank account, depositing and withdrawing as necessary. Daily, I work to deposit emotional currency and to build up my assets in our joint account. I strive for trust, honesty, integrity, authenticity, communication, and reliability. And for those times and days when I need to make a withdrawal, I do so, knowing that I have enough in the bank to withstand the current challenge. I frequently feel like I spend much of my life depositing. Then there are those incredible moments when I see a deposit from one of my children: like when I receive thoughtful, handmade, expressive birthday cards or when they wash the dishes without being asked. Most recently their deposits have appeared as text messages or as passing remarks in a conversation. Now, I can actually see the fruit of my labor ripening. It's a good thing that I learned patience.

And to you, dear reader, thank you for taking this journey with me. I hope that by sharing my experiences you will be prompted to reflect on your own lives, your own relationships, and your own growth.

May you be blessed with the courage needed to parent the best that you can.

May you be blessed with insights and inspiration from the *siddur*, enabling you to glean wisdom from our Jewish tradition.

May you be blessed with children who are happy, healthy, confident, compassionate, and loving, and who work to make our world more equitable and just for all.

Afterword

Writing this book over a 10-year period was a labor of love. If truth be told, it started out as a way for me to remember stories about my children that I thought I might forget. Once I decided to turn these stories into a book, my intention was to be able to share it with my kids when they became parents and had children of their own. Never in a million years would I have anticipated that these stories would serve as a memorial for my eldest son, Yossi, who died on February 14, 2019.

My life has been turned upside down and the stories about him are now read with a new lens. I often ask myself, would I have parented him the same way if I knew that he would die at 20? Would I have been less strict? Would I have let him get away with more? Would I have nagged less? So many questions swim around in my mind.

Here are the words (raw and unedited) that I shared with our community at his memorial.

It is hard to know where to start when writing a eulogy for one's child. It is perhaps the most unnatural of events for a parent to outlive their child.

Today there is less justice in the world.

There is less light.

There is less kindness and compassion.

There is less brilliance and intellect.

There is less music.

There is less laughter.

There are less pranks.

There is less curiosity.

There is a gaping hole that has been created, a hole so huge that it will never be filled.

AND in spite all of those huge losses, I recognize and remain eternally grateful that there have also been

more love

more prayers

more generosity of heart and spirit

more kindness

more compassion

more light generated

more…and more…and more

One of the last full conversations I had with Yossi was on January 23, 2019.

Yossi: How much longer do we have? How much longer do we have?

Ema[1]: I don't know. What do you think?

Yossi: How much longer do we have?

Ema: How much longer until what? Until you go Home?

Yossi: Yeah.

Ema: I don't know. How much longer?

Yossi: Until you go home.

Ema: No, I'm not going yet but if you decide to go, how will you make yourself known to me?

Yossi: I won't be known. I will be gone.

Ema: You know what I believe, that you may be gone physically but your soul is eternal. It will be with me always. We will always be together throughout all time and space.

I can no longer hold back my tears. He sees me crying and squeezes my hand.

I continue, Remember what Einstein taught us. He was a really smart man, right? Energy is never destroyed, it merely changes form. So you will always be—that most magnificent, eternal part of you will always exist. Do you understand what I'm saying?

Yossi: Yes.

Ema: How will you make yourself known to me?

Yossi: I don't know. I will let you know.

Ema: Ok, I'll be waiting for your answer.

Yossi: "I don't know" he said, staring into space.

Ema: What are you looking at?

Yossi: I'm waiting for an answer from that man.

Ema: What are you waiting for?

---

[1] Ema is Hebrew for Mom and is what my kids call me.

Yossi: I don't know.

Ema: Tell him you're waiting for a miracle. Now.

Yossi: Okay.

Well, clearly that miracle never came in the way that we all wanted it to.

But as one of my wise teachers, Reb Hanna Tiferet Siegel wrote to me, "Yossi was the miracle." In reflecting back on the miracle of Yossi's life, here is what did come:

Josef Lavi Pessah was a mover and shaker even in utero. In my eighth and ninth months, Aryeh and I would sit on the couch and have an 11 p.m. rollercoaster show. It was quite something. That kid never sat still. We sat entertained by these incredible moves and shifts wondering who was this kid and what would he be like when he emerged from the womb?

Well, true to form, he was my kid who never sat still, was always moving, full of energy and life, full of curiosity and incredible intelligence. I remember when he was about 18 months old and I was explaining to him that he needed to put his hand on the door of the closet and not the crack in the middle to close it and he understood. It only took one explanation and he got it. Being my first, I didn't realize that it was unusual for a child that young to have such incredible depth of understanding. That should have been my first clue that my boy was something special.

As he entered pre-school and kindergarten, as many of you know, Yossi was not one to follow rules. In fact, over the past few years, he shared stories about things he did as a youngster that I was not aware of... and trust me, that's a good thing. He was often the ringleader, playing pranks and not always listening to his elders. Following authority was not something Yossi was known for. He always, always, always marched to the beat of his own drum. Let's just say, I was on a first name basis with all of his teachers, school administrators and principals. Yossi was not an easy child to raise—strong-willed, strong-minded, stubborn, determined and brilliant—a challenging combination for any parent. I always felt like I was barely one step ahead of him.

In fact, it was Yossi who put me on my spiritual path. While I had always been interested in the metaphysics as a young child, it was Yossi who put me on my current path of meditation, mindfulness, energy worker, spiritual director and now rabbi. It was either figure out a way for me to calm and connect to the Truth of Who I Am… or resign from my parenting job. I'm glad I chose the former. One of the greatest lessons I learned from him—in an attempt to raise him with patience and love— was the message I continued to receive over and over again—whenever I felt that I had reached my limit, that I couldn't take another moment without losing my cool, I asked the Highest, Wisest part of me, what can I do to parent him better? I would hear a whisper saying, "Love him even more. Love him even more."

And that is precisely what I did.

I loved him even more.

When he got into trouble, I loved him even more.

When he reached small milestones, I loved him even more.

When he finally found his passion in guitar, I loved him even more.

When he punched a hole in his bedroom wall and wrote some unkind words about Aryeh and I in sharpie on that precise wall, I loved him even more.

When he began high school, I held my breath that this time I wouldn't be on a first name basis with the principal, I loved him even more.

When he ordered a book on computer hacking from Amazon and I asked him what the bleep was that for and he assured me that in order to help the good guys, he would need this information, I loved him even more.

When he told me that he had hacked into the school's computer system to arrange for the computer to do his homework for him, I told him that probably wasn't the best idea and he assured me that he couldn't get caught because of some computer blah, blah, blah, IP address, blah, blah, blah, and then I loved him even more.

When he only completed his homework to the most minimal of his abilities, because he had calculated down to the decimal what he needed in each class to maintain an A- average, I loved him even more.

When he didn't show up on time to his guitar recital and he told me the teacher wouldn't even notice and I reminded him that his whole life he'd always been a red Corvette and that he was the only student ever to be accepted into the Advanced Guitar class as a newly arriving 9th grader

—that his teacher would surely notice his late arrival, and then I loved him even more.

When he graduated high school with honors, when he won the Senior Fine Arts award for Guitar and for Spanish language, when he taught himself Italian by hanging out with his Italian friends, when he brought home numerous international students who were away from their home and provided them with an American family, when he donated his time and talent to numerous fundraisers—playing with his band to promote Autism Awareness, Emy's Promise, and others, when he was inducted in the National Honor Society, the Spanish Honor Society, when he was accepted to the University of Miami in the College of Arts and Sciences and decided on his own to move himself into the College of Engineering without letting us know until after he had been accepted, when he called and texted his grandparents regularly and made lunch plans with them on his own, when he served as such a wonderful, loving role model for his younger siblings and cousins, when he gave of his own hard-earned money to charitable organizations, well, as you can see by then it was easy...I loved him even more, even more.

On the last birthday card I got from Yossi, he wrote the following:

The outside of the card (a piece of white paper folded in half) reads: I was gonna draw a picture but realized I'm not an artist, so I drew you a painting of white, positive energy coming your way.")

An excerpt from the inside reads: "I wanted to dedicate this birthday card to thanking you for not only raising me these past 18 years but for caring for me, teaching me, spending time with me, helping me, the list goes on and on. But the thing that I want to thank you the most for is your unconditional love, something I've yet to master. No matter what stupid choices I made or trouble I caused, you've always loved me and I don't think that I can thank you enough for that....so thanks..."

This past year, when he got sick and confused, I loved him even more.

When he needed a North Star, I was with him every single day, every step of the way, shining light and loving him even more.

When his brilliant mind began shutting down, when his memory failed, and all that was left was his sweet, kind, precious essence, his glorious neshama (soul), I loved him even more.

And when he departed this world—at 12:21 a.m. on February 14th—I have to believe it is because I loved him even more.

We all loved him and he us.

The love that Yossi Pessah gave and received in his too short life surrounded him, suffused him and carried him home.

May that love continue throughout all time and space, radiating up to the Heavens, coursing through the Universe and back down to into each of our hearts.

And what of the grief and loss that we all feel so painfully?

Francis Weller writes that "Grief says that I dared to love, that I allowed another to enter the very core of my being and find a home in my heart. Grief is akin to praise, (as Martin Prechtel reminds us). It is the soul's recounting of the depth to which someone has touched our lives. To love is to accept the rites of grief."

My dearest, sweetest Yossi-pie, I painfully accept the rites of grief because I have always, always, always loved and will continue to love you even more, even more, even more."

After much reflection, I choose to focus on his words to me about feeling unconditionally loved to help me answer my own questions. While I believe it is natural to have doubts about how we raise our children, ultimately, I do not think that I would have raised him differently because I always loved him…even more, even more.

And I know that he felt it deeply and authentically.

May Yossi's name be for a blessing.

May the stories of his life serve to teach us.

May he always be remembered with love.

Acknowledgements

The village that it took to bring this book to light has been extraordinary.

First, great thanks to Larry Yudelson, editor-in-chief at Ben Yehuda Press. Larry and I collaborated together in the late 1990s when I wrote copy about Jewish Family Education for The Memorial Fund for Jewish Culture's website. Who would have thought that we would have connected in this way over 25 years later? I am grateful to him for believing in the message and importance of this book.

To my book designer and dear friend Peleg Top, for his creative genius and deep friendship. We met while discussing the best kind of magic markers with which to write and now, so many years later, you have created this magical cover. Thank you for capturing the essence and message of this book.

To my book mavens for sharing their experience and guidance: Debbie Fischer, Bobbie Hinman, and Judith Klau. Sending immense gratitude and appreciation to Sam Wiser, grammarian extraordinaire, as the final outcome of this book is due to your precision and editorial talent.

To Rabbi Reuven Kimmelman for his suggestion of the book's title. Fortuitously, we met one afternoon in January 2017 while sharing a car ride. He suggested the idea; I tweaked it, and I promised him that if I used it, I would give him a shout-out. Thank you, Rabbi Kimmelman!

To my amazing teachers and colleagues who have supported me and read parts of the manuscript, some even in its entirety: Rabbi Leonard Berkowitz, Rabbi Richard Camras, Robin Eisenberg, Reb Elliot Ginsburg, Reb Ruth Gan Kagan, Rabbi Marcia Prager, Rabbi Jack Riemer, Dr. Linda Thal, and Rabbi Elana Zaiman. Your comments and support helped motivate me to continue in the midst of uncertainty and moments of doubt. If I inadvertently left anyone out, please accept my apologies; it was not my intention.

To my soul sisters near and far, my life would be lonelier and far less loving without all of your beautiful souls. You are by far the BEST friends with whom anyone could be blessed: Annie, Carolyn, Corin, Dara, Hava,

Helena, Judy, Marianne, Nicole, Noga, Shanti, Shari, Shoshana, Stephanie, Susan, and Tania.

And to all of my Aleph peeps, especially Caryn, Diana, and Irwin, who supported me, especially during our time in Monsey, with much brainstorming, laughter, and guidance.

To my rebbe, Rabbi Daniel Siegel, who taught me about prayer from a Jewish Renewal perspective and who edited the book in its entirety. Thank you, my dear teacher. I remain grateful for all of the learning we have done together thus far.

To my amazing family of origin: my parents, Dale and Norty Grossblatt, for creating the most nourishing soil in which a girl could grow and flourish. You have always been my number one fans and I am forever grateful to you. Love you more than the sun and the moon and the stars in the sky. My siblings and their families, Jodi and Josh Saunders (Aliza, Bella, and Sophie) and Elise and Steven Grossblatt (Maya, Juliette, and Samuel) for your unswerving support, love, presence, and laughter. You guys are the best.

Thanks as well to my husband's family, who have become mine: Carol and Morris Lewitter, Gabriella Pessah and Adam Benson (Jacob and Risa). A special acknowledgement to Paula, Roger, Jaron, and Rachel for their never-ending well of kindness, love, and support. As well, a huge hug and kiss across the ocean to all of my Israeli relatives, who are much loved but too numerous to list.

With deep love and appreciation to my grandparents, on whose shoulders I stand: Bessie and Louis Tucker and June and Ervin Grossblatt. I remember you. I thank you for watching over all of us, those on This Side and those on the Other Side. I love you and promise to keep your memories alive.

To my incredible nuclear family: Aryeh, Yossi (z"l), Eitan, and Bat-Ella. First and foremost, to each of my kids for granting me permission to include their stories in this book. And more importantly, for gifting me with the honor and privilege of being their "Ema." They are truly my greatest teachers. To the love of my life, Aryeh: You exemplify all that is good and kind in our world. You have stood by my side, cheered me on, motivated me to finish writing, and read, re-read, and re-read. You complete me. I love you beyond all time and space.

About the Author

Amy Grossblatt Pessah has been a Jewish educator for over 30 years. Since receiving her Master's Degree in Jewish Education from the Rhea Hirsch School in Los Angeles in 1995, she has served the Jewish community in a variety of settings, ranging from formal to informal, religious schools, day schools, synagogues, camps and JCCs, and in a multitude of demographics—ranging from pre-schoolers to nonagenarians, with a special emphasis on adults and families.

In 1998, Amy became a nationally certified Jewish Family Educator and served as the Pearlstone Director of Jewish Family Education at the Center for Jewish Education in Baltimore. There she worked as a consultant to rabbis, principals, and teachers helping them integrate Jewish family education into their institutions. Amy's passion for Jewish family education was expanded through her additional training at the Whizin Institute in Los Angeles. As part of her work in Baltimore, Amy created family education programs and publications that were disseminated throughout the Baltimore Jewish community. In addition to her family education work, Amy served as a Jewish educational consultant to the Aspen Jewish community and other Baltimore area synagogues, helping them with grant writing and educational organizational restructuring. During her time in Baltimore, Amy was instrumental in creating the Jewish Family Education Network and taught a course on Jewish Family Education at The Baltimore Hebrew University.

Amy's work has been published in two Jewish Family Education anthologies: *Growing Together: Resources, Programs and Experiences for Jewish Family Education*, edited by Rabbi Jeffrey Schein and Judith S. Schiller, and *Jewish Family Education: A Casebook for the Twenty-first Century*, edited by Rachel Brodie and Vicky Kelman. In addition, Amy contributed to *Beginning the Journey: Toward a Women's Commentary on Torah*, edited by Rabbi Emily H. Feigenson, and *Irreconcilable Differences? A Learning Resource for Jews and Christians*, edited by David F. Sandmel, Rosann M. Catalano, and Christopher M. Leighton.

After moving from Baltimore to South Florida, Amy taught parenting classes at the JCC of South Palm Beach County. Later, she became a teacher for the Florence Melton Adult Mini-School, teaching both parents and teachers about Jewish values, traditions, rituals, and history. In 2004, she became the founding president of Congregation Shaarei Kodesh, where she helped build the community from the ground up. Amy wore many hats as a Jewish educator, creating the infrastructure for the religious school and the family education programming, as lay clergy, leading services and delivering regular divrei Torah, as fundraiser, strategist, marketing/publicity, and community builder. Today the congregation has grown to 200 families.

For the past 20 years, Amy has focused much of her energy on creating and nurturing her own growing family. As the parent of three teenagers, Amy has lived and breathed intimate Jewish family education. She credits her family as being her greatest teachers. An integral part of her parenting has included study and practice of Jewish mysticism, mindfulness, meditation, and music. While raising her children, Amy became trained as a Jewish Spiritual Director from 2009-2011 and in 2014 she began rabbinical school with Aleph: Alliance for Jewish Renewal. Along the way, she wrote and recorded a CD of original music chants that has been sold across the country. In January 2019, she became an ordained rabbi through Aleph.

As a trusted and sought-out spiritual leader, Amy has been leading services, officiating at lifecycle events, providing spiritual direction, teaching, and consulting. She believes that Jewish wisdom can provide access to a life filled with joy and meaning. Through her book, she hopes to transmit the depth, breadth, and relevancy of the sacred Jewish prayer book to its modern readers.

CPSIA information can be obtained
at www.ICGtesting.com
Printed in the USA
FSHW011600150420
69193FS